I0415363

The Gift of Being a Highly Sensitive Person

A practical guide to awaken the Empath within, turn your sensitivity into a superpower and stop narcissistic abuse from ruining your life

© Copyright 2019 Avery Hayes All rights reserved.

The content contained within this book may not be reproduced, duplicated or transmitted without direct written permission from the author or the publisher.

Under no circumstances will any blame or legal responsibility be held against the publisher, or author, for any damages, reparation, or monetary loss due to the information contained within this book. Either directly or indirectly.

Legal Notice:

This book is copyright protected. This book is only for personal use. You cannot amend, distribute, sell, use, quote or paraphrase any part, or the content within this book, without the consent of the author or publisher.

Disclaimer Notice:

Please note the information contained within this document is for educational and entertainment purposes only. All effort has been executed to present accurate, up to date, and reliable, complete information. No warranties of any kind are declared or implied. Readers acknowledge that the author is not engaging in the rendering of legal, financial, medical or professional advice. The content within this book has been derived from various sources. Please consult a licensed professional before attempting any techniques outlined in this book.

By reading this document, the reader agrees that under no circumstances is the author responsible for any losses, direct or indirect, which are incurred as a result of the use of information contained within this document, including, but not limited to, — errors, omissions, or inaccuracies.

To my father

Table of Contents

Taking the Evolutionary Leap: How Empathy and

Introduction

Before we can even begin to explore all the various elements of what it means to be an empath, we first need to define and understand what an empath is. So, what is an empath?

An empath is someone who absorbs the thoughts, feelings, and emotions of others. *To have empathy* is to be able to feel what it is like to be another, whether that be their current mood, emotional frame of mind, specific energy, or mental state of health. In its positive expression, empathy can be used as a gift to help others and connect to them on a humane level. In its negative expression, however, it can be very detrimental to the self, allowing the empath to pick up on things they do not necessarily wish to.

In these chapters, we will look at the main struggles of an empath in daily life, why they are harmful, and how they affect all levels of being. We will also define and integrate how empathy can be an asset if mastered, and how it can be used to develop both self and others. We will look at what it means to be a highly sensitive person (HSP) and how this, in turn, can be a gift, and finally take the evolutionary leap and connect to how empathy and sensitivity can be used to enhance extra-sensory perception, unlock spiritual gifts, and activate consciousness.

Each chapter contains real life, practical, down-to-earth and accessible guides, tips, and techniques to implement in daily life. Remember, empathy is a superpower, not a sensitivity!

Chapter 1

Defining our Understanding

The Main Struggles of an Empath

As briefly explored in the introduction, an empath is someone who takes on the feelings, thoughts, and emotions of others. They are particularly sensitive to external environments, people, situations and places which, if unbounded, can lead to anxious and nervous tendencies.

If you are reading this, then it means you or someone you love is an empath, or you believe yourself or them to have empathic tendencies. *Everyone is empathic* to some extent, as everyone is capable of empathy, the ability to feel what it is like to be another.

Empaths can be affected more severely than meets the eye. If we, assuming you are an empath, still have not learned to strengthen *chi*—the life force energy—stay centered and have healthy boundaries, we will be open to many struggles in daily life. These struggles include relationship issues, emotional problems, disruptions and issues in work, studies or career, and social worries.

Most empaths suffer to some extent in social situations until they *strengthen their inner chi* and learn how to protect themselves. Protecting oneself is, in essence, having boundaries and learning when it is necessary to strengthen your *aura*. It is putting a protective barrier around yourself. The aura is very real and is known as an *electromagnetic field,* or an *energy field* in scientific terms. As an empath, you are in tune with subtle levels of thought and energy, so you feel and experience things much more powerfully than non- empathic people. When someone may need ten different pieces of scientific information to prove something as real, you can feel both naturally and intuitively, and experience directly. This is a key piece of information to be aware of and something that should never be suppressed or overlooked.

Thoughts are powerful, and science has shown nowadays that *mind affects matter*; our thoughts vibrate outward to shape, create and influence physical reality as we know it. Just as snakes sense sounds through their tongues through the vibrations emitted, and dolphins can communicate through the waves and speak telepathically, us humans are capable of—and already have—*special communicative powers* which transcend beyond the physical realm and the five senses. Many empaths, in this respect, are natural healers, intuitive and natural counselors or therapists, or on a *soul level* have a unique purpose of being of service in some way (we delve into this perspective in later chapters).

So what are the main struggles of being an empath? Well, as one, you should know!

It all comes down to *sensitivity*. We are all sensitive, but us empath's take the meaning of sensitivity to the next level. Ultimately, the fundamental issue is that we have not yet found ourselves. When we examine all the various real-life implications and situations where an empath suffers, the only reason we suffer is because we are open to other people's energy, thoughts, and intention. We have not yet *focused our own energy within.*

The best analogy to use is being like a boat out at sea. The sea is vast, infinite and deep. The ocean's waters are a beautiful reflection of us, our souls and the inner workings of our psyche. Yet if a boat sails across with no sense of direction, no intended destination and no means to steer, what will happen? *The boat will get dragged around by the tide!*

This is, in essence, why all empaths suffer before evolving and why some of us still suffer. On a personal level, I am an empath. I pick up very easily on other people's energy and emotions and, until I learned how to become strong and centered within, used to suffer. Going out in public and social situations, specifically public transport like buses and trains, was a truly terrible experience. The main thought that ran through my head, repetitively, was: 'What do people think about me?' The main belief that I had ingrained into daily existence was that 'everyone was interested in me,' like I had to *put on a show* and *be everything for everyone*. Traveling was a horrific experience.

When we stop to think about this, one couldn't get any more ludicrous! If we are *all one*, one consciousness and one global community, then surely every single other being will want to live life without nervousness, stress-free and peaceful to go about their daily life. No one is that interested in me as they, based on the ultimate goal of wishing to be happy, healthy and free from suffering, wish to *be themselves* and be free to do whatever they wish to do during their journey.

This is how powerful our thoughts are. We create and shape our realities based on the energy, thoughts, and beliefs (and intentions) we give them. So this *illusion* created held no significance and, ultimately, I did not need to suffer.

It is important when looking at how and why we empaths suffer that we consider its opposite, its duality. When we are not interested in how other people affect us, we are in a state of *creation, actively shaping and influencing* the world around us with our own thoughts and stories. Or we are, at least, attuned and aligned to our own story, our *own unique blueprint, frequency or daily reality*, which for an empath with a unique inner beauty and love for the natural world can be a divine and blissful experience.

Being an empath is not just connecting to other people's thoughts, emotions, and energies, but it is also being influenced by them. An empath subconsciously responds to other people's intentions, and intuitively feels and perceives others. They can also perceive physical sensations and hidden spiritual urges, in addition to invisible motivations and intentions. In this sense, you cannot fool an empath because they simply know when you lie, deceit or have false intentions.

There is a *karmic element* to being an empath. Empaths subconsciously and unconsciously take on other people's karmas. This links with collective wounds and ancestral traumas, which we will explore in-depth later.

Let's now explore the main struggles of being an empath and how extreme sensitivity affects us in daily life.

Relationships

To be an empath in relationships can be extremely difficult. As you are aware, empaths are extremely sensitive to their surroundings and feel emotions very intensely. It is a natural desire of the empath to heal and generally try and make another's life less hard. As empathy is a quality associated with *feminine energy*, empaths often take on a motherly role, the role of the caregiver. Of course, this can be positive and lead to many beautiful interactions, connections and experiences;

however, one of the shadow aspects of the motherly energy is smothering.

Because an empath does not know where the self ends and begins, boundaries can be a problem. The innate desire to heal, help and be sensitive and considerate to other's needs can be overbearing and simply too much. If the empath is in a relationship or partnership with other empathic, intuitive and sensitive signs such as water signs, or other signs with strong elements of water in their charts, then this may not be too much of a problem. However, with a lot of people, a healthy sense of independence is essential, and too much of anything can lead to serious problems in relationships.

With loved ones, family and friends, it can be very difficult for the sensitive empath who takes on the feelings of their loved ones. Even when they have (finally) found their joy, are happy, and in a light-hearted frame of mind and being, something could arise which automatically burdens them. It is impossible for an empath to *not feel*, to not merge with another and experience what they are going through to help them through it or to take on their pain. This is why empathy can at first be seen as both a curse and a blessing. As you will see in later chapters—it is *not* a curse!

Furthermore, in family and friend relationships, the 'normal' expectations, duties and responsibilities of a sensitive empath can be overbearing. Simple tasks which may be simple and easily performed by non-empathic people require a huge amount of energy. This is because empaths are in their element in the natural world, in nature, around animals or with those sensitive and introspective souls who connect with them on their *empathic wave*. Because empaths feel and experience life with depth—*on a much deeper level* than the majority of us—the constant expectations of family can really pull an empath out of their alignment and, once this happens, it can take a long time to find themselves again.

Music, nature, art, beauty, reflection, silence, stillness and introspection are activities all favored by the empath. As an empath, you have a huge heart and are highly attuned to both your senses and your intuition. Your intuition is your *inner knowing*. This means that you can often be a magnet for unsavory personalities, narcissists and energy vampires. In a western society not nurtured in the right environment, unresolved traumas and wounds can build up and affect all your relationships later in life.

Suppression of emotion is a major problem for the empath. Because you take on so much from others, and sometimes aren't even conscious of it, your vessel becomes 'full' with other people's stories, feelings, and problems. This can lead to health problems, some minor, however, some more significant. As we function as a whole or holistic being (we explore this in depth in the third section of this chapter) blocked or repressed emotions lead to not only physical ailments, but also detrimental mental patterns and spiritual ill-health. Physical problems associated with an empath's highly emotional and sensitive nature include aches and pains, muscles tension, stored and trapped emotions manifesting as back, neck and shoulder problems, weight gain or weight loss, stress, anxiety and inability to sleep, and ill-health or disease.

In love and romantic relationships, the empath is prone to those orientations of smothering and mothering love, as previously mentioned; however, they can also pick up on things much deeper. We often have yet to heal our traumas, our *collective and subconscious wounds* which lie beyond the surface. People grow up in a western society without the sense of family, intimacy and connection that others, such as in shamanic and tribal communities, have. We do not meditate or practice mindfulness, and we do not have certain values and understanding integrated into our conscious mind from a young age. Traumas and wounds, therefore, grow with us as we grow up and, by the time we start exploring our sexual, romantic and intimate desires, we have brought unresolved issues into our relationships.

Unless you happen to be blessed with a yogic, mindful, tantric dance-teaching, empathic and wise, heart-centered being as a partner, these unresolved traumas are present in *all* relationships!

Relationships are a *mirror* of ourselves and until we do the inner work necessary, which takes time and is a journey, either: 1. we will continue to *project* unresolved traumas on our partners or 2. we will *pick up* on theirs. Of course, as one grows older and starts their own path to self-mastery, relationships change in that we become more conscious, loving and in alignment with spiritual and higher values. Until that time, however, those with an empathic nature will continue to attract those who need healing on some level, because we empaths naturally get drawn to the broken, the wounded, or to those who need fixing.

Empaths attracting narcissists and energy vampires is a foundational element to learning what it means to be an empath and to begin the journey to self-mastery (finding your superpowers). Now, if you know what a narcissist is, then this statement should start to evoke some pretty strong emotions and memories. Narcissists, as you may be aware, are the complete opposite to empaths in that they are *inherently selfish*. They seek to take, whereas empaths seek to give, therefore, when it comes to the empath-narcissist relationship, an empath will spend a lot of time in pain, despair and suffering. This is mainly due to your need to please; you genuinely are happy to appease, please and sacrifice. Unfortunately, however, as a taker and abuser with a *highly manipulative personality,* narcissists abuse your kind nature and, furthermore, inflict suffering, sometimes to vast extents. Energy vampires are literally this. They *drain your energy,* and your inner beauty and weak boundaries are targets for their own nature.

Unless both narcissist and empath have begun their self-development journey and began to heal themselves and their own wounds, these relationships involve lots of trauma and great suffering for the empath.

Careers

At work, the empath is naturally sensitive to his or her environment, other people's moods, hidden thoughts, feelings and intentions. As it is the natural tendency for the empath to wish to help in some way, it can be difficult to balance the practical and detail-oriented aspects of the job at hand with a desired connection and 'helpful friendliness' with colleagues. Empaths do not necessarily struggle with practical tasks—I know many empathic and sensitive people who thrive at work—it is just that they tend also to want to take on other roles at work which *can* be detrimental to the job at hand.

When we refer to the wish of wanting to 'take on other roles,' we are specifically speaking about the nature of the empath being the healer, counselor and compassionate friend in need. People with a strong empathic nature tend to play the role of caregiver, therapist and counselor, which can, of course, be seen as a good thing; they are beautiful qualities! Yet in the workplace, if one does not have a profession specifically related to the caring, healing or coaching-type professions, or creative and artistic, then this may have a detrimental effect on career progression and development and the ability to perform practical tasks.

In a positive light, however, it is important to note when delving into the struggles of an empath that being *the friend in need* in the workplace can be very beneficial to one's place in the team and could in some cases lead to promotion and increased opportunities. Therefore, as we will explore later, it is essential for you as an empath to *unlock your natural gifts* and align with careers, paths and choices which best define your nature. We explore all this throughout the rest of the book.

School

It is important when looking into what it means to be an

empath that we integrate an understanding of our experience (or our children's experiences) from school. Being an empath growing up can be extremely difficult, specifically with the already existing pressure to perform and achieve top grades and skills. Adding an empath's heightened sensitivity and ability to feel the feelings of everyone else into the already present teenage problems everyone suffers whilst learning and growing, self-confidence, self-consciousness, shyness and interaction with peers, can create a very emotional and introverted young adult!

This is an integral struggle that empaths face growing up: introversion. As briefly explored, an empath loves the natural world and feels truly *at home* when with animals and nature. This is because animals and nature don't expect anything from them, they are free to just *be themselves*, be quiet and feel safe and happy in their own thoughts. At school, however, there is very little time for this sort of activity and behavior and, combined with some of the strong and fierce personalities of non-empathic children, a young empath journeys into adulthood with a lot of hidden and repressed emotions and 'wounds.'

This, of course, affects all relationships from work, careers, personal goals and dreams, stepping into one's true path, and love and family relationships.

As empaths are more inclined to pick up other's feelings and project it back without being aware of it, young empaths *bottle up emotions* to the point of unexpressed emotions leading to *traumatic experience.* Also, empathic children also feel particularly suppressed by oppressive structures, both at home and in other situations. Young empaths, therefore, need space and freedom to roam, express themselves and be accepted. They thrive in the abstract and need to be around non-manipulative people in order to be their true selves, grow and develop. If they are not allowed to express themselves abstractedly and creatively and are also shamed or judged continuously, this can lead to rejection, low self-esteem and depression.

As it is part of the empathic personality to have a natural aversion to violence, loud noises and excessive radiation, such as television, young empaths growing up often don't understand why they feel the way they do. They are *very sensitive* and any images or scenes of emotional or physical pain or suffering can have a traumatic effect. As not all parents or guardians are empathic, this quality is simply not understood; therefore, the child grows up with *repressed traumas* and a lack of wisdom or emotional maturity on what is occurring on a deeper level.

Another main problem that links with this is that they are

often told to 'stop being so sensitive.' As this is just who they are, this can lead to low self-esteem as mentioned and a feeling that they are not allowed to be who they are or feel what they feel. These suppressed issues are then taken into adult life, and the beautiful gifts of the empathic nature are prevented from being nurtured.

In the final section of this chapter, there are practical tips and exercises exclusively for children to use either at home or to help during school time. If you sense your child is an empath, or simply highly sensitive and introverted, please don't be hesitant to share them!

Why is Ungrounded Empathy Harmful?

Ungrounded or unbounded empathy is harmful because we are not *protecting ourselves* from those intentions or energies that may be harmful. As explored in the first part of this chapter, not all people, places or situations are harmful; sometimes it is just our illusionary fears and mental patterns. Sometimes, however, there really are 'bad people,' toxic relationships and those who seek to harm, judge or persecute.

As an empath, I am sure you know all too well how every time you achieve happiness, success or achievement in life or simply are 'in your flow,' someone comes and attempts to disrupt this. Yes? Well, this is because you *naturally attract narcissists*.

Now, I am not suggesting the world is against you, because it isn't. But due to your inherent nature, there is a *subconscious* part of you that invites negative, detrimental and harmful energy into your life even when you do find your happy place and seem to be in a beautiful and abundant flow. This will happen until you heal it fully and do the work necessary on an *inner level*. Until an empath reaches the stage where they are fully in their divine flow, self-autonomy and natural power, leading their best life, there are still deeply ingrained beliefs, thoughts and conditioned patterns which will keep leading to the interactions and experiences one does not wish to attract.

Later in this book, we will explore how ancestral wounds and deep trauma profoundly affect empaths and how these wounds and traumas intrinsically shape and create the person we know as 'the empath.'

Unbounded or ungrounded empathy is one of the main causes of the struggles and sufferings us empaths face today. What does it mean to be ungrounded?

To be grounded is to be protected, secure, safe and connected to our environment and the word in which we live. Being grounded brings a sense of security, of connection, and of *awareness*. Just like in my sharing of how I used to feel in public transport due to my highly sensitive and empathic nature, being ungrounded is being disconnected from your body and natural surroundings.

The mind and body are completely connected, just as the mental and physical planes of existence work, or are supposed to work, in harmony. Empaths tend to *overthink* and create stories and realities which are not actually there. It is like having your head in the clouds without the dreamy and euphoric feeling. Of course, empathy in its positive expression can do exactly this!

So, regarding those 'bad' and toxic people who actually do wish to bring us down: Not having healthy boundaries and awareness can be very detrimental to the self. When I say that you naturally attract narcissists, there is actually great beauty in this. The whole essence of an empath is one of *connection*, of intimacy and *feeling one with* another.

When an empath has embraced and aligned with their gifts, as we will explore later in this book, they naturally embody 'the healer,' 'the counselor' or 'the one with uncompromising compassion.' Empaths are natural healers, lovers and helpers at heart.

So, of course, when your energy is open and unprotected with no clear focus or sense of direction, narcissists are naturally going to gravitate toward you. An empath, as you are aware, is all about giving, a sense of sacrifice (to a healthy extent) and being there for others. We possess great sensitivity, empathy (of course) and care and compassion for others and the natural world. Narcissists, however, are selfish and primarily care about what they can take.

We empaths can learn a great deal from narcissistic characters, or those who wish to cause us harm; as like with any hardship or struggle in life, it can make us stronger. To do this, however, we first need to recognize, to re*cognize* why toxic relationships and scenarios are manifesting in our lives, and how to heal the inner workings of ourselves, which inevitably manifests externally.

Boundaries: The Personality Types You attract

Boundaries are your new guardian angel!

Just as you have programmed your mind to think thoughts and believe illusions that cause you suffering, becoming one with the term *boundaries* and practicing them on a daily basis could be one of the most powerful and loving things you do for yourself.

When we have boundaries, we literally put up an invisible barrier. This barrier is for all the b*llshit! It is an invisible but energetically real line that says NO to your time, love and energy. It keeps your space as your own and allows your truth, your utmost highest-vibration self to stay centered and aligned. *To align* is to become centered with, to become *in tune with* and have your focus and energy directed toward.

It is very important to note, however, that having boundaries is not putting yourself in a bubble. One does not close themselves from the world, new experiences or loved ones. The boundary is for the narcissistic, abusive and harmful people and situations. It is an energetic circle, if you will, that speaks to the world: *"only loving, beautiful, connected and positive experiences welcome. Please leave your rubbish and abuse at the door."*

Once again this isn't about closing yourself off from the gifts of your empathic nature; you can and will still be there for others who may truly need your help.

This invisible circle is also your canvas. By closing yourself off to all the potential negative, harmful and detrimental energy, you are *creating a space* for new experience, connections, and opportunities. These can manifest in the forms of relationships, educational opportunities, work blessings and opportunities, or any other area of life. When we close ourselves off and say no to the experiences, feelings and thoughts we don't want, we *actively attract* abundance, bliss and prosperity in all aspects of life.

In later chapters, we will explore the positive effects associated with boundaries and creating space; however, for now, let's look at specific characters and personality types that may be manifesting in daily life.

The Narcissist

As mentioned, narcissists simply wish to take. They don't care about your feelings or well-being in any way, shape or form. How they treat you does not concern them. They also only choose to see the 'bad,' the *dark or shadow aspects* of both life and you. You could literally be shining in front of them and they would still not see it, or appreciate it. Your real, beautiful qualities such as kindness, care, empathy, generosity and compassion are wasted on them and, in addition, they will twist things around. Narcissists are *highly manipulative* and will drain you of your love, energy and resources.

The Abuser

Unlike the narcissist who simply doesn't care, the abuser actively causes you pain. They thrive in your upset, suffering and despair, and your characters are polar opposites. Just as you receive joy from helping others and allowing your kind and compassionate side to shine through, abusers receive pleasure from inflicting pain on others. Although it is important to note that this is *not* their true self. Abusers are very much in their ego and paradoxically really need the help of a loving and supportive empath (although this doesn't mean you should give it to them. We will explore *discernment* later).

The Jealous One

These characters are self-explanatory. They just can't be happy for you and although they may pretend, fake and smile in social situations to appear in a good light, they really aren't and never will be happy. The qualities that make you real are secretly despised by them because they wish to embody what you possess and have not *evolved* past the egotistic, separation-based nature, which makes them jealous. Jealous characters are one of the main reasons empaths find it very hard to find happiness in life and they can make you feel guilty each time you do.

The Persecutor

Persecutors take things a step further than the abusers, as their desire to cause you harm is unconscious—it runs deep. These people have a *deeply ingrained belief in their psyche* which goes past the day-to-day. Just as Christ was crucified on the cross and witches were burned at the stake, persecutors have an inherent 'block' against the empath's nature. Furthermore, the block can also manifest as *real vindictiveness,* a very dark and shadowy aspect of the self which runs deep in our collective conditioning. As empaths are all about depth and a persecutor's issues run deep (on a soul level), persecutors can be influenced by an empath's love and care. It usually takes real, deep and soulful displays of genuine compassion and a desire to heal to do this.

The Cynic

These people simply don't believe. No matter what you do, regardless of what you achieve, it simply can't be true. Cynics will never allow you to shine in your truest and most beautiful light, as they just refuse to see you. The reasons may be many, such as a lack of self-worth or love for themselves which they project outward, or because of unseen resentments and jealousies, to name two examples. However, the fundamental point is that it is physically impossible for you to be who you say you are.

One of the main struggles of an empath on their journey to self-mastery and finding their superpowers is to develop healthy discernment, boundaries, and learn to protect the protective energy field and stay centered. As natural lovers, caregivers and peacemakers with an inner beauty that radiates out, these types of characters are magnetic for the unprotected empath. Learning when to say no and practice *healthy selfishness* is an important aspect of the empath's journey.

Daily Implications: Exploring the Different Bodies of Existence

What do we mean when we refer to the different bodies of existence?

We have a mental body, a physical body, an emotional body, and a spiritual body. We also have an astral body and, extending further, the soul or the oversoul. This is the part of us which is connected to the collective consciousness, the *shared* aspect of our Self which exists beyond time and space and beyond this specific lifetime.

In many schools of thought and practices, specifically those related to ancient cultures and healing modalities, it is believed that all illness and disease begin at a *soul level*. Any and every ailment, issue or imbalance is believed to have its origins in the *disharmony of the mind-body-spirit connection*. Just as our mind affects our emotions and emotions affect our physical health, all of our bodies are connected and have a profound effect on one another.

In the Reiki System of natural healing, for example, healing takes place on the *ether*, the energy body just above the physical body. It is taught and practiced that illness and disease begins on the ether and manifests in the physical; therefore, any energy work applied to the etheric body will subsequently have a positive effect on the physical body (which of course in turn affects, mental, emotional, and spiritual health). This is because all illness stems from the mind. Disease is the body or mind being at dis-*ease* with itself. All illness, therefore, is said to originate from imbalance.

The findings of *kirlian photography* support this. There is a fantastic study which directly measures the physical effects and presence of *chi* (as cultivated by martial artists and energy healers), which we explore later.

How does this relate to being an empath?

An empath overthinks, as previously discussed, and has irrational, neurotic and psychological thought patterns, which are detrimental and not helpful. Empaths also suffer from afflictive and inharmonious emotions and, generally, see people and the world as separate from them. This is very contradictory as an empaths' true nature as you are aware is empathic, you see and feel the world, people, animals and all of nature as one. Yet cold, harsh and abusive personalities can lead the sensitive empath to close themselves off from the world and pollute their beautiful and connecting way of viewing life. So, where do these distortions come from?

Although we empaths have natural and rather powerful empathy, the distortions in our thought patterns are due to our sensitive nature to other people's 'stuff,' the wounds and collective conditioning. These distorted thought patterns thus affect emotions. The emotional body then becomes *disorientated*, absorbing the stories and projections from everything and everyone around you. There is *no focus* or sense of direction, like the boat at sea, so you get pulled around with the current instead of steering the current, or, at least, yourself.

Simultaneously this 'stuff' can manifest as others' judgements, distorted perceptions, and cynicism toward your gifts, which has a profound effect on your ability to experience them. This is until you learn how to protect yourself and center, of course.

Taking a Deeper Look at Distortions of the Different Bodies

All life is designed to work in harmony. Just as we are connected to the sun, sea, air and earth, and they are connected to each other, our own *bodies* are designed to work in harmony and function as a whole, as a unit. We refer to the term 'bodies' as this implies that there is more than physical reality and a three-dimensional way of being and perceiving. Space and time are complex elements and science has shown how all sorts of *extra*-sensory phenomena exist in an energetic universe. Of course, as an empath, you already know this!

Everything is said to work in a state of *vibration*, of *frequency*. Just as sound waves and particles vibrate at different speeds, so do colors, objects and things in the natural world. So do we. Scientists have actually made objects levitate through sound and acoustic vibrations alone and, as you may be aware, many animal species exhibit all sorts of incredible gifts. The earth herself is intended to function as *one living, conscious entity* where all the interacting parts are conscious and aware of one another. Our bodies are intended to achieve and maintain homeostasis.

These truths show just how interconnected and unified we are supposed to be.

So when it comes to the empath, everything that does not operate in harmony with its self, the self—the holistic and fully functioning person—is said to be in *a state of distortion*. We live in a *uni*-verse and *extra*-sensory gifts and abilities are as natural as all things *super*natural. The qualities are just enhanced and evolved.

Language itself is a powerful shaper and creator of the empath's views, beliefs and thought patterns, as the struggles we see are based on the *stories* we tell ourselves every day. A story can be seen as any belief, reality, programming or conditioning we tell ourselves are real. Without stories, life would simply have no meaning, no truth, and no sense of direction or focus.

Here are some brief ideas into the types of stories we empaths tell ourselves:

- 'Everyone is thinking about me or looking at me. I am expected to be on show, or try and be something for everyone.'

- 'I am expected to always find intelligent, interesting or fun things to talk about. I need to be my best for everyone 24/7 and I am not allowed to relax or be at peace for myself.'

- 'Everyone expects me to sacrifice myself, my health, my wealth, and my sanity. My joy and contentment are not as important as everyone else's.'

- 'People always expect me to bend around their will. I am just here to appease and please others.'

- 'I am finally happy, successful and in flow! Am I doing

something   wrong? Now I need to put all my time and energy into helping others with great sacrifice to myself.'

- 'No one wants me to be truly happy or successful. I am being selfish.'

As you can see, and feel, these stories are very discomforting! These *distortions of the mind* all stem from extreme sensitivity and sensitivity overload and imbalances in the different bodies. As an empathy, you essentially feel you need to pick up, tune in and respond to every single person, animal or natural entity in your immediate environment. Over time, people, places and situations become stories and before one has fully integrated what is actually occurring you have become everyone's empath. *Being everyone's empath* has some seriously negative consequences as shared in 'the main struggles of an empath.' It can affect every aspect of being.

Let's now look into the distortions of the different bodies in greater detail.

The Mental Body

This, of course, is our mental plane of existence where all thought arises. Now, as our mind, body and spirit are designed to work in harmony, connected to and at one with itself, distortions of the mind can be seen to have their origins from any and all of the other bodies. On a soul level, if our ingrained beliefs are particularly distorted, out of tune with the natural world and universal way of being, then our thoughts will be greatly influenced. On a physical level, if our divine vessels are unhealthy, out of balance or suffering from any particularly disruptive illnesses or ailments, our mind will be affected. Emotionally, if we suffer from emotional discord and disunity, then this further affects our mind and the thoughts we have.

Our thoughts and beliefs, therefore, greatly influence our lives and the state of health of all other bodies. Depending on whether we use our minds positively to empower, enrich and attract beautiful experiences and interactions in our lives, or negatively with harmful and detrimental *stories*, being empathic can be heaven or hell.

In the next section of this chapter, we will look at various ways to help live life in a state of bliss, unity and connection, free from the repetitive and unhealthy mental patterns.

The Emotional Body

Just like the mental body the emotional body is intrinsically connected to all of the other aspects of *the self*. Our emotions and emotional state of health influence the thoughts we have, the choices we make in terms of the foods and substances we consume, and how we physically feel. Our emotions affect the spiritual and astral bodies as if we are not in an emotionally stable, secure and connected space we are not open to spiritual connection and awareness. *Feeling* is the key regarding all of our choices and how we live out our relationships, careers, personal projects, and daily excitement and happiness.

Just as with repetitive thought patterns, being stuck in *cyclic emotional patterns* will keep the same stories on repeat, disallowing you to move forward in life and attract new opportunities, blessings and experiences. One of the main gifts of an empath is the ability to connect to others and feel what they are feeling, distortions in one's emotional body can prevent an empath from accessing their own true purpose, path, and sense of passion. Most empaths choose professions or activities which allow you to help others in some way, or at least make yourself emotionally available in daily life, to connect to others on a real and empathic level.

The gift of the empath is, therefore, to be able to tune into other people's emotions, possessing extreme *emotional maturity*. Until one has developed this within themselves and *accepted both the light and the shadow*, the beautiful and not so favorable qualities within the self and in life itself, unresolved emotional patterns and repeat emotional distortions will continue to manifest.

The spiritual body

The spiritual body is the place where all spiritual, extra-sensory and psychic stimuli and gifts arise. Clairvoyance, clairaudience, clairsentience, telepathy, extra-sensory perception, and deep empathy all come under the realm of spirit. Everything has a spiritual essence, as everything has an *energetic* essence; the whole universe is governed by invisible and unseen forces. Depending on the way one perceives and the meaning they wish to give, becoming in tune with the spiritual body is very easy.

In essence, being spiritually aware or being connected to the spiritual body is perceiving and being open to the subtler realms of existence. It is about feeling, being an active participant in daily life and choosing to experience the world and all it has to offer in a way that is connected, in harmony and *at one with* the natural world. It also extends beyond this as it is in the realm of spirit, where all psychic phenomena as described can be accessed.

In terms of the other bodies, if there is a disruption in the spiritual body, this will have a profound impact on mental and emotional health. If one does not see from a loving, compassionate and interconnected way of being, then thoughts and emotions will be subsequently influenced. Feeling *spiritually connected* to both ourselves and the world

44

around us provides a sense of peace, love, and inner contentment and connection; therefore, distortions in the spiritual body can also have a negative effect on our physical well-being. Problems such as overeating, comfort eating, choosing the wrong foods, and generally not giving our bodies the love and respect they deserve link strongly with spiritual ill-health. As an empath, you are naturally more in tune with the spiritual aspects of being (even if you are not currently accessing them); therefore, disconnections from spirit will affect you more severely than others.

Later we will explore the purpose, power, and potential paths of the empath nature.

The Physical Body

The saying 'your wealth is in your health' holds great truth. When our physical bodies—our divine vessels—are out of sync, this greatly affects all other aspects to our being. Thoughts, emotions, feelings, and the ability to connect to the more subtle and spiritual aspects of life are deeply affected. We may become heavy, lethargic, unmotivated or immobile. We may become stressed, anxious on a daily basis or suffer from nervous tension. Anyone of our physical body's systems, immune, digestive, circulatory, skeletal, or nervous/neurological systems may become disrupted.

The body sends signals and impulses to the different parts of itself. These neurotransmitters literally transmit data, information and sensory stimuli to all different aspects of the brain and the way in which it works. As the brain is responsible for receiving stimuli and *making sense* of all the information received, an imbalanced and unhealthy physical body can have a negative effect on our emotions, sense of joy, ability to learn and process information, and all other aspects of life.

In terms of connecting to and enhancing unique gifts, if there is a problem in the transmission, the message will be disrupted. In other words, we won't have the synapses or connections available to tune in to subtler levels of perception and awareness.

Treating our physical bodies with the love and respect they deserve, therefore, by eating whole foods, lots of fruits, vegetables and herbs, and eliminating toxic foods, such as sugars, processed and artificial chemicals and preservatives, can have a very powerful effect on our mental, emotional and spiritual health, and ability to thrive and survive as an empath.

Your wealth is in your health!

Practical Tips and Techniques

At Work

Work can be stressful, especially when bombarded with infinite concerns, tasks, and duties and feeling other people's energy. A simple yet effective technique to try at work, therefore, is to take time throughout the day to recharge yourself and replenish your energy. This is essential as, as an empath, you function at a much higher vibrational frequency than most. You, therefore, unconsciously absorb and respond to all the impressions, thoughts and feelings around you which can, of course, un-center yourself.

Throughout your day, either during your breaks, when you go to the restroom, or if you have a quiet moment by yourself, create a chi ball. This may sound like something from Alice in Wonderland, but it is very real and powerful!

Simply close your eyes, breathe, and calm your mind. Bring your awareness inside and hold your hands up to your heart, palms facing each other. Breathe deeply into your hands and envision a ball of glowing, loving energy (chi) inside. Watch it expand, actively feel it. There is no need to rush—these few minutes are for you.

Once your breath is steady and you can actively see and feel a ball of beautiful golden, swirling energy in between your hands, set an intention. This intention can be anything that will bring you what you need, such as 'I am at peace, I am calm, I am centered and I am safe.' You can also intent individual qualities into your chi ball, such as peace, focus, protection, and bliss.

Finally, bring your ball of chi up slowly and pour it over your heart or over the top of your head. Watch it, envision it, filling you with the quality you have just charged it with. Say thank you to the beautiful and loving life-sustaining energy that has just filled your being with calm, focus, and positivity.

This can be done in any work environment and can have a super effect from as little as 3- 10 minutes!

Chi has been recognized by ancient cultures for thousands of years and is currently cultivated daily by millions of people around the world. Martial artists work with chi for their health and vitality. Chinese medicine also embraces the positive effects of chi for longevity and healing. Chi is essentially your *vital life force* responsible for energy levels, mental and emotional health, and the free flow of energy through the body. It is increased through conscious breathwork and is essential to cultivate as an empath with such high sensitivities to other people's thoughts, emotions, cynicisms, judgements, and, in extreme cases, abuse.

In Relationships

In relationships the main way you suffer as an empath is due to your over-sensitivity and inner feeling that you need to always be your best or help in some way. This leads to the imbalance, as mentioned in 'The Main Struggles of an Empath.' So to help with this, try this easy yet highly wonderful technique for feeling more connected to and at one with your partner, friend, or family member.

During a conversation or interaction, when you begin to feel tense, discomfort or like your sensitivities could get the better of you, *visualize a golden light* over their brow. Now, this is actually much simpler than you may originally think. It is effortless to perform, as your mind naturally wonders and can connect to the subtler levels of perception and reality with ease. Therefore, you can do this with your *inner mind and inner awareness* whilst still maintaining eye contact.

The brow area is also known as your 'third eye' to many cultures, schools of thoughts and philosophical teachings. It is the center of consciousness, spiritual insights and enhanced and psychic perception. Envisioning a golden light over this area in your mirror will help immensely. You will start to feel more relaxed, less stressed, and feelings of oneness will increase. Your body should begin to loosen and you will feel comfortable, and as if you don't have to 'put on a show' or be anything but your natural self. It can also bring feelings of light-heartedness and genuine joy!

The visualization doesn't have to be golden, it can be any color you want to enhance the qualities of. For example, if you envision a green glowing light, this relates to the heart (the color of the nature with strong associations to empathy, love, and kindness), and can help with feelings of love, warmth and kindness, caring and compassion (which you possess naturally). Visualizing a yellow light can aid in confidence and positive feelings due to the 'sunny' nature of the color and orange can enhance feelings of warmth, comfort, and emotional connection.

Visualizing a blue light may help with your ability to communicate and express yourself with ease and free from tension (due to its strong associations with the sea and sky, which have a calming and peace bringing influence); simultaneously, purple, indigo, and violet have a 'majestic' feel and will enable you to step into your divine empathic power, intellectual wisdom, and intuition.

The power of color is recognized by many, and as an empath with a deep connection to both nature and your subconscious, using this visualization exercise to aid in your relationships and self-confidence can have great effects.

At School (Youth-orientated)

As the main problems for empathic children during school are over-sensitivity, a tendency toward introversion and a lack of focus and concentration (due to their daydreamy nature), the best tip and technique to suggest is to learn how to increase their *inner fire*.

As empathy is an inherently feminine quality, and empathic children can be overly watery and yin in nature (which relates to sensitivity and emotions), this is often an imbalance of the yin and yang, lunar and solar qualities within. Making a conscious effort to increase one's inner fire, therefore, can help drastically.

This exercise is both fun and effective, and is similar to the visualization above for adults in relationships. Get your child to envision a snake. First, ask your child to think about the qualities of a snake, how they sense vibrations through their tongues, how their bodies glide effortlessly and smoothly along the earth, and remind them that the snake is a symbol for kundalini energy, the energy which flows up the spine. Educate them on the energetic nature of the snake and all it embodies, and then ask them to envision it. Really *become* the snake

During school, again either at breaks or in their own space in the restroom, perform a short breathing exercise where they imagine their body like a snake's and breathe chi- life-force energy—up their spine to the top of their heads. They should imagine that they are the snake, and they can sense people's thoughts through the air and that earth is their true home. They should also visualize a ball of glowing golden light at the top of their heads as they do this.

This snake meditation is simple yet beneficial to increase a young empath's inner fire, and can also help them feel more connected to others and their environment by increasing their feeling of connection to others and the natural world. Children have an incredible imagination and empathic children even more so. Any visualization exercise which allows them to use their unique sense of imagination and deep intrinsic connection will allow them to thrive!

When Dealing with Narcissists

The best way to deal with narcissists as an empath is to just not take them too seriously. Quite simply, you don't need to get involved with their drama. As there are a lot of people who have narcissistic personalities, and often you have shared friends or family, transform your knowledge into *humor*. Don't let yourself get affected and try to raise them up with your energy and ways. Of course, ideally you do not want to associate with real narcissists, however if in a situation where it is a necessity—laugh! Bring humor and lightheartedness into the conversation. This way, the energy will be directed toward a positive light.

Another profound way to deal with a narcissist is to increase your sense of personal boundaries, which we explore later. As previously mentioned narcissists gravitate to you like a magnet; therefore, having strong boundaries can help overcome any and all problems associated with their toxic personalities.

When Dealing with Abusers

With abusers, it is essential you protect yourself. Unlike the narcissists, as discussed, these people genuinely wish to cause you harm, pain and suffering. It is important to put up your protective boundaries and stay strong within.

Advice: Practice daily affirmations and mantras to strengthen your mind. We explore the science of these later; however, for now, they are extremely powerful and effective for strengthening your mind and keeping you strong and true to yourself. Combined with self-healing exercises, such as meditation and mindfulness, you will better be able to put up an energetic barrier to their 'stuff.'

Always remember to have love and respect for yourself. You

deserve better!

When Dealing with Jealous Types

Kill them with kindness! OK, maybe don't kill them. But creation and destruction are both fundamental elements of life.

To deeply jealous people, killing them with kindness is on some level a destruction of their world. The reality they have created comes into question and their illusions break down. The best way to deal with a jealous personality is to *be your beautiful, bright, compassionate and empathic self*. Remind them with love and humor what they've got going for them and *alchemize* their negative expression into a positive one. Make the conversation about their fortune, success, talents and gifts, and allow the spotlight to be on them. In this sense, you are *holding space and shining your inner light* and, although it may appear that they have 'won' and you are just appeasing them, you are in fact in a process of self-mastery. You are allowing your true nature of empathy, kindness and compassion to shine.

So let them shine! But always be aware of your silent power and the energies playing out behind the scenes.

When Dealing with Persecutors

Persecutors need healing, and a lot of what they do and say is unconscious. There are many ways you can live, interact and be around persecutors successfully and without losing yourself. Each will depend on the individual.

The best way is to suggest and introduce activities you know make them happy. This is specifically for friends and family (if you cross paths with strangers who want to burn you at the stake, simply walk away). This is because there is a deep and buried unhappiness and traumas present in persecutors. They see your empathic nature and the beautiful qualities which make you so, and instinctively go on the attack or defense.

The issue runs deep, and it is most likely wounds and unhealed traumas that have accumulated throughout lifetimes.

The problem, therefore, lies on a soul level. Yet as daily life is not just about the soul, people make choices and experience bliss from mental, emotional, and physical stimulation, the best way to thrive and survive as an empath around persecutors is to do what makes them happy. We are all intrinsically connected and sometimes your way and your likes aren't the only way.

If you can learn to balance and harmonize your personality with theirs and give a *healthy amount of sacrifice you* will find that life around a persecutor becomes much easier. You will actually begin to appreciate one another.

All the empathic activities you love and hold true, such as going out for a walk to connect to your favorite tree, will be respected and allowed as you have allowed them to be, too. You can also actively vibrate thoughts of love, compassion and healing when in their company.

When Dealing with Cynics

As cynics simply don't see you, the most appropriate way is to simply *stop caring*. As an empath, you care deeply, so this may be hard at first, but recognizing and *accepting* that their minds are programmed a certain way can lead to a blissful existence.

Be yourself and don't worry about what they think or believe. This is a great character-building exercise and way to be as it allows you to *stand in your truth* and remain wholly and completely true to yourself. By being yourself, you are actively showing them the beautiful and unique qualities of an empathic nature and secretly *inspiring them*, even if they seem unresponsive. Be inspirational!

Another profound way to connect to your empathy and strengthen your resolve simultaneously is to recognize that you are here to show a new way. You are inspiring, dear empath, and although 'man was created equal,' we are *not* all the same. You have unique ways of seeing, perceiving, and experiencing reality, and can therefore raise others up to new heights, offering an integrated and holistic dimension to any shared activity or interaction.

We are all students and teachers, and regardless of your follies or sensitivity and boundaries issues you are one of the more evolved types of people among us. Once again, not many people can connect on the rare level in which you can and a cynic who questions or doubts you is clearly not empathic. Being the teacher to others whilst remaining the humble student to yourself could be one of the most loving and empowering things you do.

Strengthening and Protecting Your Mind

Mental Re-programming Exercises

The most effective way to reshape the remaining mental structures and thought patterns which affect you negatively are to include a number of mind reprogramming exercises into daily life. This can be done by receiving the help of qualified and experienced professionals, such as cognitive behavioral therapists, hypnosis therapists and neurolinguistic programming therapists. All of these, however, can also be practiced on your own.

Every day before going to sleep, dedicate half an hour to an hour of mental reprogramming activity. This involves the following:

- Binaural beats, which are frequencies of sound which have specific effects on the brain. They can be played and tuned into to receive a specific effect, reshaping neurological structures which are responsible for thoughts, awareness and all aspects related to the mind (which has a profound effect on the rest of self).
- Lie down and place your left hand on your stomach and your right hand on your heart. Set the *intention* of allowing healing energy to flow through you and harmonize your mind, body, and emotions. Connect to the energy of the binaural beats and focus on your breath. Feel your hands warm as they begin to channel chi—the life-force energy—while keeping your awareness on your inner levels of being. Allow the sounds to drift you off into an altered state of being.

This is a very powerful exercise and can be used for a range of effects.

Binaural beats having an intrinsic effect on your neural system and subsequently affecting thought, feeling, and levels of perception is backed by much research; however, one profound study to support this was published by *Front Psychiatry*, who found that binaural beats and auditory stimulation actively affected both cognition and mood.[1]("Auditory Beat Stimulation and its Effects on Cognition and Mood States," 2015)

This is especially useful as an empath to know as until you find your flow you can be prone to the 'dark' aspects of life and being. It is natural to go through low moods from time to time, however, unfortunately, you absorb everyone else's low moods, pains, wounds and traumas. This means that any proven and useful tool- in this case binaural beats- to enhance your mood and cognitive functioning abilities will significantly improve all aspects of your life.

Strengthening and Protecting Your Emotions

Meditation

Just like the visualization exercises explored earlier, focus on your stomach area. This area is known as your sacral and dantien or 'center of chi' to some. Your sacral embodies your emotions, your sexuality and your creativity. If there are any blockages in either one of these three aspects to life, the others will be affected. Meditating on your sacral, therefore, can help increase a healthy flow of chi through your body and release

---

[1] Auditory Beat Stimulation and its Effects on Cognition and Mood States. (2015). Retrieved from https://www.ncbi.nlm.nih.gov

any stored or repressed emotions.

This is particularly effective for letting go, transcending repetitive detrimental emotional patterns and healing any repressed wounds. As you are aware, as an empath who functions at a high emotional frequency, exercises which focus on your sacral area—the region responsible for your emotions and intuition (hence why your intuition is often called your 'gut' or 'gut feelings') are essential. Use the visualization exercises combined with breath and meditation to heal your sacral region and allow your empathic self to shine in its truest light.

In addition linking to exercises like meditation and visualization is *mindful meditation* specifically on your intuition. Intuition is an inherent part to being an empath— you can't separate them. Learning about unique and self-evolving techniques to connect to your intuition will allow you to thrive as an empath, instead of being 'dragged around by the current.'

Strengthening and Protecting Your Physical Body

Eat healthy! Transitioning to a vegan or whole foods diet can have some powerful effects on your ability to thrive as an empath. Confidence can increase, you can feel lighter and connected to your heart and true self, and you generally can be surer of your worth, gifts, and abilities.

When we eat healthy, high-vibrational whole foods, our physical vessels become lighter. This, in turn, affects our mind, emotions, spirit and empathic nature. Food such as fruits, vegetables, beans and pulses, nuts and seeds, herbal teas and purer versions of the foods you may like to eat have a deep physiological and psychological effect on the nervous system. As empaths tend to suffer from self-consciousness, over-sensitivity, and nervousness from time to time, eating the right foods will improve all aspects of life.

Handy tip: Cut the sugar! Sugar is one of the main causes of stress in the body and mind, and is especially harmful to an empath's sensitive nature.

Tip for Entertaining Small Talk

Many of you empaths have difficulty entertaining small talks and talking on the phone due to your sensitivity. It can be hard to remember to just *take it easy* with a constant need to be your best, come up with interesting conversation, or shine the light you know you hold inside. For this reason, it is good to remember that, especially with friends and family, they love you regardless! Remember each time you are on the phone or in social situations that '*they are a reflection of you.*' Say it in your mind like a mantra until you retrain your brain and adopt this new level of awareness.

You can also combine any of the visualization techniques for the desired effect.

Chapter 2

Empathy as a Gift

Empathy as a Gift: The Start to Self-Mastery

As briefly explored in chapter one, empathy is a great gift once we have done the inner work and come to terms with our follies. As with all life, there is no light without dark and no shine without shadow. The day cycles into the night just as the night spirals back into day.

In this respect, one of the main blocks on the path to embracing the beautiful qualities of being an empath, and starting the journey to self-mastery, is that we have not accepted our *shadow*. Just as we explored in 'the emotional body,' us empaths possess incredible gifts of connection and intimacy. It is through *feeling* that we truly connect to the empath's gifts and subsequently thrive in all aspects of life. How can we expect to step fully into our powerful, sensitive, and empathic nature if we choose not to feel?

The key is to know what not to feel and when to have discernment. In chapter one, you learned about why and when you should put up your barriers, protect yourself from others and the world, and close yourself off to external influence. However, in this chapter, we will delve into when and why we should *open ourselves up*, allow our sensitive side to shine through, and allow ourselves to feel fully.

With narcissists, abusers, jealous ones, persecutors, and cynics, there is a need for protection, for discernment and healthy boundaries. However, an integral part to the empath's journey, as you will discover, is that once we have healed ourselves on all levels, and become strong and centered within we can then use our sensitivities for the benefit of others. Instead of passively drifting along with no clear sense of focus or directed awareness, we can be the *creators*, actively influencing and changing the world around us for the better.

This, in essence, is the ultimate goal of the empath. To align with the unique gifts and qualities and exist in our highest possible frequency, our best sense of expression can arguably be seen as the purpose of the empath and its manifestation can present itself in many ways.

Let's explore these ways deeper.

How can it Be Used to Enhance the Self?

Empathy can be used to enhance the self in many ways. All aspects of life can change as soon as you become in tune with your natural self and learn to stop attracting the magnetic negatives of your nature (narcissists, the energy vampires, etc.). Let's look at these at face value.

- Confidence

- Artistic and creative abilities

- Autonomy, responsibility and maturity

- Creating one's own structures

- Self-respect

- Healthy boundaries

- Following one's dreams

- Ambition, goals and aspirations.

- Intimate relationships

- Optimum health

- Self-mastery

- Self-worth and belief in one's innate gifts and abilities

- Inspirational

These are just some of the positive expressions of the gift of empathy; however, the list can arguably be seen as endless. This is because you can, literally, connect to the self, to the whole person, in a way which is *multidimensional*. Any and every element to life and human nature, therefore, can be tuned into.

Any aspect you feel you need to increase can be achieved through your *deep connection to your inner worlds and rich emotional wisdom and maturity*. Your self is comprised of your mental body (mind), emotional body (emotions), physical body, and spiritual body (spirit). Empathy and the empathic nature can act like a *bridge* to any hidden aspects of self that needs bringing to light, or if you simply are lacking in something or need to heal.

When we refer to empathy acting as a bridge, this literally means it can be seen and used like a *subconscious superpower*. Just as you feel things that may not be able to be explained by the rational mind or logic, you experience life abstractedly, philosophically, intuitively, and with *all* your senses. To increase any aspect of yourself, all you need to do is set your intention and use your deep empathic nature as a superpower to heal or enhance whichever element you feel the need to. For example, say you are lacking in confidence; a mindfulness or mantra meditation would come very natural to you. You would remind yourself of those times you were fully in your beautiful and divine nature and used this to help someone else, either through your words of wisdom, unique insight, compassionate heart or patient and genuine listening abilities. You would then *connect* this memory and feeling to the quality of confidence. Thus, any and every quality, characteristic or energetic frequency you wish to connect to and integrate into daily life and the self can be done, and almost effortlessly. Your empathic ability to feel and connect on a deep level can almost be seen as a real superpower.

It is a *super* power!

How can it Be Used to Enhance Others?

As we explore in-depth in chapter four, as an empath you embody unique characteristics and energies which, are ultimately beautiful gifts (see 'Healers, Therapists and Spiritual Intuitives). In addition to the *inner archetypes* of 'the healer,' 'the caregiver,' 'the counselor,' 'the animal activist,' and 'the spiritual intuitive and psychic,' you also possess gifts and abilities which lie in the realms of the artistic and creative, paranormal, dreams, imaginative, and shamanic/the seer.

In this section, we will explore these aspects of the empath nature further.

The Inner Artist

You are an artist! You see and create beauty in everything, the trees, plants, animals, stars, planets, and universe itself. To create art is to capture and translate beauty, an essence, emotion, memory or story. You do this naturally.

Empaths make incredible painters, poets, artists, musicians, storytellers, and filmmakers. You can tell the story of an object, being or place through photography or expressing through the written or spoken word, and have a unique gift for sharing your appreciation for art and beauty with others. Many are naturally drawn to empaths for your inner harmony and love of beauty and combined with your ability to merge with another on a deep level, you can use this in any chosen artistic pursuit.

Musically, empaths have an ability to enter transcendental, or trance states and can experience any and every emotion of a song, even if it doesn't particularly relate to your own life. You become one with the music to the point of embodying the emotions, story, frequency or reality being played out. If you choose to express this through dance, you can heal both yourself and others through your powerful sense of expression. If you sing, chant, or play an instrument, this can be used to not only entertain but uplift and inspire others.

If expressing yourself through poetry or the written word, you bring through unseen and often genius ideas, archetypes and concepts for collective learning and evolution. Essentially any art form you choose can produce some incredible creations.

The Paranormal Investigator

An inherent part of your nature is the ability to experience all sorts of paranormal, psychic and extra-sensory phenomena, which many people take years to become familiar with. These can also be developed and enhanced with practice, self-mastery exercises and a continuous intention to connect to your true nature for your and other's highest good.

Lucid dreaming, astral projection, psychic mediumship and channeling are all natural skills of yours. With lucid dreaming, you may often find yourself being awake in dream states and being conscious and in control of the dreamscape in some sense. You may discover that astral projection comes effortlessly, and you merge into and out of different states of consciousness and transcendental awareness as easy as breathing. This is because your mind is so attuned to the collective, the subconscious and the subtler realms of perception. Astral projection and lucid dreaming, therefore, may be a norm in daily life.

You may also find yourself drawn to mediumship, channeling higher wisdom, knowledge or power for the benefit of others, or delving into the realms of spirit and spirit communication. Due to your ability to merge with another on a soul and spiritual level, any activity or practice regarding the paranormal, psychic and spiritual comes naturally and, with the correct training and teachers, could be developed and perfected as a way to be there for others. Your natural empathic tendencies, therefore, can be allowed to shine in their brightest light through connecting to these inner archetypes.

The Dreamer

You are a dreamer! All empaths are dreamers. This can manifest as having your head in the clouds, daydreaming, and feelings of transcendental awareness on a daily basis, with actively dreaming being a major aspect to life. There is not just this physical realm, and your true nature allows you to explore dream worlds and altered states of consciousness at will.

Astral projection and lucid dreaming, as described above, tie into this.

Furthermore, as an empath with the ability to connect to a higher power, the divine or source, you can use these gifts to become a conscious dream explorer and interpreter. This essentially means practicing certain skills and working with dream herbs, gemstones, and the universal life-force chi, to connect to and develop your gifts further.

Once achieved you can navigate dream space consciously and see dreaming as a way to receive wisdom, direct insights and messages, and connect to any spiritual helpers or guides for daily assistance. Through meditation and daily practices, you can then actively use this gift for helping others, connecting to them consciously and being a channel and guide for their subconscious.

It is a very powerful gift to possess!

The Imaginative One

As your mind is free to wander, roam and explore all that is, many empaths have great imaginations. In addition to all the above your skills lie in the realms of storytelling, advanced listening skills and ability to understand others, and the potential for genius creations, concepts and ideas. You are a natural at bringing through other worlds and alternate universes, and your ability to articulate them and communicate them effectively makes you a unique artist, creative, musician, writer, poet, storyteller, performer or actress/actor.

Many empaths use this gift to teach or to work with children; however, it can also be evolved to create some revolutionary 'big ones!'

The Shaman/the Inner Seer

All empaths possess a natural seer-like quality. This is due to your link to the shamanic and spiritual realms. A shaman is someone who is in tune with spirit, connected to and at one with the trees, plants, animals, unseen worlds and universal energy. They use a variety of tool to connect to the invisible elements of reality and do so for healing, both personal and collective. As an empath, you have a natural inner shaman and seer.

Shamans are also referred to as medicine men or women in that they work with herbs, sounds and instruments, the earth, flowers and plants, and maintain a direct link to source or spirit through their intentions and daily practice. Naturally, this could sound like I just described the empath!

In this respect, therefore, there could be no greater gift than connecting to your shamanic and seer-like essence to help others on their journey. Empathy is a beautiful quality to possess, and in an often cold, hard and separation-based world, shamanic living could be a blessing to many. It is certainly not something that should be repressed or watered down for cynics!

Some unique characteristics of the empath personality:

- *Telepathy*: you have the ability to read people's thoughts and see inside their minds. This can be used for all sorts of healing, psychic work, counseling or compassionate fields, and the creative and imagination calling professions.

- *Psychometry*: many empaths can receive information, knowledge and insights from objects. You literally 'tune in' to the vibrational frequency of the object, or photograph, and this can be used in service to others.

- *Mediumship*: you can feel and connect to the presence of spirit and unseen entities.

- *Intuition*: you possess a highly developed intuition and inner knowing. This can be used as a gift in many ways.

- *Clairvoyance*, *clairsentience* and *clairaudience*: as an empath, it is natural to be able to know, feel, see, and sense things which cannot be explained by the rational mind. You see beyond the surface and can use this to be of help through spiritual counseling or coaching, channeling and acting as a guide, and any activity or field related to psychic phenomena.

- *Precognition and precognitive dreams*: you can see the future! This makes you a natural visionary, seer, psychic, shamanic or spiritual healer, and artistic creative.

- *Animal whispering or communication*: many empaths can speak to animals in such an extraordinary way, it is often viewed as magic! Animals are highly empathic and sensitive to our intentions, thoughts and energy, therefore becoming a guardian and whisperer of animals is a great way to share your empathic gifts.

- *Psychic, physical and emotional healing*: you literally take on other people's 'things' as your own. Physically this can translate as actually embodying and experiencing another's physical ailment as your own. You can use this superpower to connect consciously to another's body and astral body to feel and sense what is occurring on a deeper level. Emotionally and psychically the same can be done respectively.

- *Nature*: you have the empathic ability to read, connect to and merge with nature. This can be used to benefit others in infinite ways!

Now, you may not possess all of these gifts (although many empaths do), but you should never allow any cynical non-empathic people who simply don't see destroy or suppress your unique abilities. Remember, your empathy is a superpower and remarkable in its own right. These natural abilities of yours should be *honored, cherished,* and *respected,* and just because someone else doesn't understand them does not mean they are not real.

Energy and Boundary Protecting-Strengthening Exercises

These exercises and techniques relate to the elements of the empath nature explored in this chapter. They can, however, be used for any of the other topics explored throughout the book.

Learning to Laugh

As an empath, it can be very easy to take life too seriously.

Because you are used to feeling appreciated and loved for your wise insights, warm and gentle nature and empathic gifts (once you have grown up and found those who appreciate you), there is a tendency to forget to balance serious, deep and soul-level sharing and connection with letting go and lightening up. One of the main reasons you suffer when around people or out of your comfort zone is due to your *oversensitivity*; there really is no need to be so sensitive or self-conscious all the time.

So, to help with this a handy tip, is simply this: *just learn to laugh*! Not a weird, mean or spiteful laugh (you may know *we are all one* and have a strong heart, but not everyone does). But I am referring to a real, sincere and open laugh, a laugh which recognizes your oneness in a situation.

Everyone is a reflection of you; we are all mirrors, and sometimes what is truly needed to release trapped emotions and blocked energy is a genuine, deep and real laugh. This can be very helpful in many social situations and help you to take things easy. Combined with the powerful energy exercises, you should find any feelings of anxiousness, tension or low self-esteem disappear in no time. Literally!

When you laugh, you release trapped energy and *rise* it to conscious light. A lot of what its stored is unconscious or residing in our subconscious; therefore, in terms of being an empath, your lack of boundaries and letting harmful or negative energy in may arise from not being away that you are holding on to thoughts or emotions which are not yours. Laughing *shakes things up,* and subsequently enables you to see and feel your own energy.

Working With Your Dreams or the Subconscious

We do explore the subconscious and psychological perspectives to empathy later. For now, looking to your subconscious—and in particular your dreams—can aid greatly in your ability to develop stronger boundaries and enhanced energy in daily life. As already stated you are a natural dream explorer, whether that be lucid dreaming or exploring the dreamworlds at will (consciously). It is in dreams where you have access to your subconscious and, specifically as an empath, you are better able than most to tune in to some subconscious message or universal symbolism for healing and insight.

This can affect you in so many ways and on so many levels. Any issue you may be suffering with such as oversensitivity, self-esteem or confidence issues, boundaries, problems with speaking your truth, and stepping fully into your light can be overcome and healed through *allowing* and being open to receive the wisdom inherent within your subconscious. You are intelligent as well as intuitive and your cells 'know,' they are conscious and aware. It is in dreams where a part of you becomes triggered, activating some aspect of yourself which is currently in the dark.

Other ways to connect to your subconscious include journaling, writing, expressing yourself through art therapy or music, and psychoanalysis or any holistic therapy. Holistic therapy is important for your nature, as we explore later, as being an empath is a *holistic experience*. You are not just three-dimensional.

Developing Discernment

Finally, one of the best ways to get in touch with your superpowers and live your best life is to develop discernment. Now as an empath this may be hard as you are such a giving and selfless soul, yet as you are aware this can leave you depleted and victim to the abuse and will of energy vampires, narcissists, and other toxic personalities.

Fundamentally, discernment comes through your intuition and advanced emotional wisdom. You can only access this however by being true to yourself and connecting to your unique spiritual and psychically geared gifts. Being an empath inherently involves a psychic and spiritual element as empathy is literally feeling other people's emotions and feelings and, in more advanced cases, reading others' minds! Again, we are all connected on a subtle level and empathic power is on the same wave as this.

There are many ways to develop discernment and hopefully the techniques and exercises shared throughout these chapters can help you do so.

Chapter 3

HSP's and HSI's

HSP's and HSI's: Who Are They?

HSP's are highly sensitive persons, or highly sensitive people. HSI's are highly sensitive introverts. Both clearly share the same characteristic of being highly sensitive, just like the empath; however, there are some fundamental differences.

An introvert is the opposite of an extrovert, someone who *goes within* more so then they go without. Highly sensitive introverts do not necessarily become fearful, although they can—of others or social situations—they just genuinely tend to feel happier and more comfortable in their own energy. HSI's are symbolized by being reflective, and enjoying activities that are introspective, contemplative or antisocial in nature. When in social situations, they tend to *go inside*, not being the life and soul of a party or gathering, but being the quiet one who observes, reflects, and listens. They live in a world of senses, connected and attuned to the subconscious.

Introverts can often have a very rich inner life.

Observation is a huge element and fundamental part to the highly sensitive introvert's existence. To others surprise, they genuinely find joy and inner contentment in silence. They live in a world of thoughts, impressions, and hidden emotional responses and beliefs, and *attune to* the subconscious aspects of reality, the layers 'behind the scenes.' They feel comforted there.

HSI's can feel fear, experience anxiety or nervous tension, but this is not necessarily a rule. Being a HSI can be seen as a negative, depending on the way one wishes to perceive introversion; however, to view being a highly sensitive introvert as something inherently negative would mean one has their own issues and repressions to work through. This, of course, can work in two different ways as 'feeling happier and more comfortable in their own energy' is also something the HSI has created. The truth in itself that they have needed to *create a persona to protect themselves from their own sensitives* can be viewed as not particularly positive.

As with everything in life, reality is full of *projections*; we project every day. These projections onto others and the world itself manifest as thoughts, beliefs, stories and impressions that only have the substance we give them. Projections can, therefore, be positive or negative.

Without judgment or over-analysis, it can be seen that highly sensitive introverts have found their protection, their direction. They are very similar to the HSP as they are highly sensitive, but the difference is that they have found a way to express this sensitivity and still interact with the world. Being an introvert does not mean that one locks themselves away in their room or is fearful of others and social situations it simply means that they choose to stay in their own inner worlds even when with friends, families, or in social gatherings. Being a highly sensitive person, on the other hand, implies that they have not yet found their 'secret shield' and that they are simply highly sensitive. This is one aspect to being a HSP and the term in itself does not give any suggestion as to whether their sensitivity is expressed positively or negatively, or whether they are affected detrimentally on a daily basis or whether they have utilized their sensitivity for creative and spiritual pursuits.

The creative and imaginative essence to HSP's is something we will go into in the next section.

So how do HSP's and HSI's relate to empaths? Well, they clearly both have an empathic nature as with great sensitivity comes considerable amounts of empathy. But the difference between an empath and the highly sensitive people is that empaths *take on* the thoughts and feelings of others, whereas the HS's are just highly sensitive to them.

Thus, life can be harder for the poor empath as we have great levels of sensitivity to external energies and environments. The HSI has learnt to align with introversion as a safety for their sensitive nature, they have found their solace. The HSP often resides in a world of vast imagination and evolved levels of creativity. Yet we empaths are still open and susceptible to everyone else's stories!

In the next section, we will explore the differences between these three personas in more detail. Even as an empath, you may feel you can relate to HSP's and HSI's in some way, therefore delving further into what it means to be each can provide an understanding for when you wish to use your empathic sensitivities as a gift.

The Difference between HSP's and HSI's and Empaths

As discussed, HSI's have found their solace in their introversion and inner worlds and HSP's can think, feel, and behave in a number of ways. As we have already described, the nature of an introvert in the previous section, let's look at what it could mean to be a HSP.

Highly sensitive people are not strictly defined in any particular way. Unlike highly sensitive introverts, who are specifically introverted, and us empaths who absorb and take on other's emotions and the like, HSP's can be characterized by a number of personas. For those artistically and creatively minded, being highly sensitive is a great gift. Like the HSI becoming immersed in another world entirely can be a haven, a heavenly space enriched with beauty, extra-sensory and psychic perception and empowerment. HSP's can be bright, creative and possess advanced levels of imagination. They can tune into subtle levels of perception, spirituality and psychic phenomena and can also be highly empathic and compassionate.

Thoughts, patterns and behaviors that may appear negative to the non-HSP may, in fact, be extremely beautiful and healthy qualities. Being sensitive to chemicals, having aversions to fumes, pollutants and manmade products with toxins, loud noises and perpetual television sounds, all may seem 'weird' or out of the ordinary to some, but to the HSP—and to the HSI and empath—these are just experiences and ways of being that *enhance the self*. Not tuning into these elements of life is a *healing process*.

Referring back to the different bodies as explored in chapter one, being highly sensitive can in reality be seen as a blessing. The whole point of life is to be happy, healthy and achieve harmony, is it not? If we are complex beings whose sole purpose is perhaps to achieve homeostasis and a perfect state of health, a holistic and mastered way of being, then there surely must be more to some of the realities and stories that are being played out in western society today?

Chemicals, food toxins, noise pollutants, excessive technological radiation and distractions, angry and aggressive personalities: these are just some of the current situations occurring in reality. So, if the HSP is sensitive to these, does it not suggest that they may actually be more evolved, healthy and *mentally clear* than a lot of people engaging in these unhealthy stories?

Life itself is an illusion and there is ultimately no right or wrong way to do anything. To be sensitive is to be *in tune with your senses*. To be out of the ordinary is to be *extra*ordinary and to have superpowers is, well, to have *super* powers!

Empaths are also prone to the same sensitives as HS's, however, we are usually too busy being absorbed in everyone else's stories before we can stop to think what is good for our health and peace of mind. Once an empath has started the path to self-mastery and learned to overcome the daily struggles associated with being an empath, you will find you become more aware and conscious of sensitivities such as the ones listed. The bodies are designed to work in harmony and we often can't become aware of certain truths, knowledge or perceptions until we have *let go of the old* and *created the space necessary* to fill ourselves up with new stories, beliefs, and behaviors for self-love.

The main difference between us empaths and those of a highly sensitive nature, therefore, is that the HS's have not yet developed and *integrated* their empathic gifts to help others and enhance the Self. HSP's may choose a path which allows them to tune in to their extraordinary creative and imaginative gifts, however, HSI's tend to live their lives in a subconscious, 'other realm' introverted space.

It is important to explore the different angles with regards to observing the nature of HSP's. In 'the Highly Sensitive Person,' clinical psychologist Dr. E. Aron suggests that although HSP's may "have been called shy, timid, inhibited or introverted... these labels completely miss the nature of their trait. Thirty percent of HSPs are actually extroverts."

She further goes on to say that "HSPs only appear inhibited because they are so aware of all the possibilities in a situation." This point brings into awareness an important similarity between highly sensitive people and empaths in that we are so open to external influence and all the various possibilities and realities in any given situation. Once again, there is no *focused awareness*.

Dr Aron further goes on to ask the following questions:

- "Are you easily overwhelmed by such things as bright lights, strong smells, coarse fabrics, or sirens nearby?

- Do you get rattled when you have a lot to do in a short amount of time?

- Do you make a point of avoiding violent movies and TV shows?

- Do you need to withdraw during busy days, into bed or a darkened room or some other place where you can have privacy and relief from the situation?

- Do you make it a high priority to arrange your life to avoid upsetting or overwhelming situations?

- Do you notice or enjoy delicate or fine scents, tastes, sounds, or works of art?

- Do you have a rich and complex inner life?

- When you were a child, did your parents or teachers see you as sensitive or shy."

These questions portray the sort of issues that HSP's face due to their implications. Of course, regarding the topic in discussion, some of these questions can be used to analyze what it means to be an empath and a highly sensitive introvert.

Here are some of the conclusions by Benita A. Esposito in 'The Gifted Highly Sensitive Introvert: Wisdom for Emotional Healing and Expressing Your Radiant Authentic Self.' Take a moment to explore how they relate to you as an empath and how you can thus tune in to the traits of the highly sensitives to help others on their own journey of transforming their empathic nature into superpowers.

The first conclusion she discusses is that emotional intimacy is in our nature. The time that we are at our happiest include moments when we can feel like we are connected to someone on a very deep level. It doesn't matter where we might be in life. There might be some things that we have to figure out, mistakes from our past we feel regret over, or perhaps a terrifying future we know nothing about. Regardless of our situation in life, as long as we, as empathetic humans, have others in our life to depend on - people we can make real connections with - we'll feel fulfilled.

We also understand what it means to be emotionally gratifying to another person. We can better understand the needs of others in our life, therefore our relationships can have greater meaning. We know how to take care of other people in a way they might not even know is best for themselves either.

She also stated that we are looking for this spiritual meaning from the moment we are young children. We are driven by curiosity, always looking to solve some of the greatest mysteries that we're presented with.

We can become easily disinterested in conversations that might not present much of an intellectual challenge. Alternatively, it can be very easy for others to open us with us because we create such a space to easily share emotional bonds.

Esposito also compares our abilities to be empathetic to how a cat uses whiskers as sensors. These whiskers can feel out others and their emotions, whether it's the feelings of people, the thoughts of animals, and the state of plants. We can take on these kinds of feelings without even having any realization we are doing so.

While it might be something that comes naturally to us, better than other, non-empathetic people around us, it is also much easier to feel overloaded by these emotions.

As empaths, we can even sometimes feel as though we're taking emotional steroids. This means that we will feel what others are more intensely, sometimes to the point where we don't know what our emotions are in comparison to the way someone else is feeling.

This can be challenging because there are some points where we might even take on too many of other people's emotions. We might be trying to help someone, maybe through their own emotional healing process, but instead of aiding them properly, we get distracted by feeling what they are too profoundly.

It will also be harder for our emotions to simply go away, as Esposito explains. This is why it will be more important for empaths to learn how to manage their emotions. If we aren't aware of the things that we are feeling, then they will start to directly impact our lives in many different ways.

If we let our emotions simply sit there and fester, doing nothing to make ourselves feel better, then eventually, they will cause us to explode. This will be at the worst possible time for the most part as well. When we can't control our emotions, then it will be a lot harder to control when they might be emerging.

We also have to pay special attention to understanding our family's origin wounds as well. The pain that our ancestors carried will trickle down into us. This is either through abuse and treatment passed down, or even just the emotional stress that they had to carry in their lives.

As empaths, Esposito knows that it is crucial that we start to communicate in a more efficient way. Emotions can be confusing and tricky to handle. If we want to fully get a grip on them, then we must start to better find ways that we can share how we feel with other people. Not only that, but we need to open communicable bonds so that others understand how they can better shar their emotions with us, in turn.

Throughout our experiences as empaths, we have been able to grow the ability to better listen to our gut-feeling. If we feel as though someone is threatening or that we don't trust them, it can be easier for us as empaths to know whether or not this is a feeling we should trust.

Empaths will also take more responsibility than they can handle sometimes, just because they can so passionately want to fix a situation. This might make it harder for us to take care of ourselves, causing emotions to be even higher and more unmanageable!

Anything that stimulates our senses can become easily overwhelming as well. Whether it's something visual, textual, fragrant, or that affects our hearing, it can sometimes be too much. Maybe you run into a person wearing heavy perfume, or the lights are just too bright in a room. When these sensory stimulants are high, it can be harder to process our emotions and really understand what's going on.

One of the biggest benefits of being an empath, however, is that we are creative. We are beautiful, passionate, emotional beings. We appreciate how gorgeous nature can be simply on its own. We are easily entertained by the amazing sights that surround us. Perhaps you simply like "people-watching," or even elevator music can be interesting at times. No matter what it is, we find expression and beauty in all around us. Even something seemingly meaningless might have a great importance to our lives.

Because of this, we process everything very deeply as it comes. Rumination, analyzing situations, and constant thoughts over what has already happened can be common. At the same time, we will look at things under a very critical eye. We can break things apart to find the deepest meaning, and we will find interconnections to other relevant information.

Because of this, we can also find it very hard to take criticism. We have trouble with certain feedback because we will think that it speaks a truth about who we are. For this reason, we might have built up our defenses. Before becoming aware of our emotions, it is likely that you had shut certain people out of your life or avoided doing something you cared about because the criticism was just too much to handle.

One of the good parts about this, however, is that it makes us more responsible people. When we see the criticism easier, it causes us to step our game up, and we'll take on extra responsibilities. We'll ensure we've done our part, and everything is taken care of.

This can result in us becoming better leaders as well. We are able to see to the end point, we can somewhat "predict the future," in the sense that we understand everything that can go wrong. We feel what those around us do, and we are prepared for the worst, so we can better lead those around us.

An empath's powers can grow so much that they might even be able to better heal others around them. They can feel their pain better than the person with that emotion might, meaning it's easier to pick out what needs to be done in order to remedy the situation.

Benita Esposito finishes up her conclusions about empaths with the ideas that we might struggle to set boundaries sometimes. We have to have the ability to be who we are, we need room to breathe, and we need to spread our wings. When we struggle to create boundaries, most of the time because we don't want to hurt others, then we end up suffering in the end. Empaths need to identify what they want and need, and effectively communicate that to others.

All of this makes it challenging to try new things every once in a while, but the better we control our emotions, the easier it will be to live the life we desire most, one where we're confident, happy, and surrounded by those we care about deeply.

'*We can get overloaded with feeling everyone's emotions*' in point three brings to light the foundation of the topic in question. The highly sensitives can become *overloaded*.

Although Benita A. Esposito shares some very on-point truths and makes clear that being a highly sensitive person is not a flaw in itself, highly sensitive introverts can hide from the world and go within to a point that they miss out on other aspects of life. They find solace in introversion as a solution to their sensitivities, which *is* a detriment in itself. This brings into awareness an important difference between the HSI and the empath.

Everyone is both introvert and extrovert to some extent; however, to close oneself off from life, from reality and all its joy and pleasures because one is susceptible to their own empathic nature is, in effect, devolving. HSI's may have created an inner world of peace, introspection and adopted a specific way of perceiving and interacting with the world, but those beautiful qualities of extroversion and actively showing up are being missed as a result. Joy, laughter, mental exchanges, learning, stimulating debate, conversation and intimate connection are all experiences which, on the whole, the highly sensitive introvert does not experience.

In this sense, and as we will explore in the next section, the empath can be seen to be more evolved than the HSI's and their personality favorable. Once empaths have embraced the gifts wishing to be integrated, it can arguably be suggested that the empath nature is where all sensitive personality types are steering, or should be steering. Unlike the empath, HSP's and HSI's find the external overstimulating and thus they feel disconnected from it. Empaths, however, represent *connection* and use empathic powers to connect to others, environments and the world around.

This is the fundamental difference between those with a highly sensitive nature and empaths. Although both feel things very deeply and are greatly affected by the ability to tune into subtle perception and a range of senses, it is empaths who *alchemize* the relationship with the external world and all its many disruptions.

We do this in a way which is healing, harmonious and synergistic, thus becoming one with the world.

How to Unlock the Empath Nature

The empath nature can be seen as a goal all sensitive people should work toward. By now you should be aware that we are not talking about fearful or ungrounded empathy, absorbing people's thoughts, feelings, and emotions in a way that is harmful to the self. We are now referring to real and *on-point* empathy.

HSP's and HSI's naturally possess great levels of empathy and are capable of making the transition to an empath in its ultimate expression. As explored in the previous section, this is the next stage in the human journey.

The empath nature can be defined by kindness, caring, compassion and the ability to connect to others on a deep level. You are considerate, intuitive and orientate toward paths of service, of helping others in some way. Even if you do not choose a profession that matches your empathic nature, you still live daily life with a specific way of perceiving, being, and behaving. You strive for connection and appreciate depth, beauty, and qualities such as love and respect.

There are more than the five physical senses, and the empath sees in a way which is multi-dimensional due to one's sensitive and spiritually orientated nature. Just like the highly sensitive introvert, you see, feel, and experience daily life through a subconscious lens, a world of emotions and underlying hidden thoughts, feelings and stimuli.

Empaths, however, also live in the 'real world' and ground the heightened sensitivity and ability to merge with another into the physical body and material realm.

In addition to having empathy and naturally picking up on other's moods, 'the empath nature' extends beyond this. It is *consciously integrating and embracing natural gifts to be of service to others and create a connection* (in its highest expression). Unlike the narcissist who wakes up and has no intentions or actions which directly help others, the empath when in their true nature views and experiences daily life with the *specific intention* of being an empath, i.e., you keep your thoughts, heart, and mind directed toward certain beliefs, stories, thought patterns and topics of conversation.

This is a very fundamental element to the empath nature: *heart*. You feel deeply and are a lover of peace, harmony and intimacy (whether platonic or not), therefore, characters and interactions which are not aligned to heart, kindness, care and compassion are a real turn off. Aggressive, harsh or spiteful personalities stand out on your radar, and you are inclined to gravitate toward kind, caring or warm-hearted souls.

Spirituality doesn't define empathy per se. However, it is intrinsically linked. Many who awake to their empathic gifts awake to their spiritual gifts simultaneously. This is because 'to be empathic' is to know what it is like to be another, to feel another's feelings as one's own and to be inside another's mind. This, of course, involves a connection. 'To be spiritually' anything is to have spirit as your ally (spirit-u-ally) and the universe does exist in a state of natural unity which implies in itself that there is a *spiritual-energetic* element to life.

Before going into how to unlock the empath nature as a HSP or HIS, let's briefly redefine it.

The empath nature:

- Kindness, caring, and compassion

- The ability to 'take on' the thoughts, feelings, and emotions of another

- The gift of 'tuning in' to another's mood or inner workings, which can be used to help, heal or offer insight

- Recognizing one's susceptibility to external influence yet staying centered, aligned and with a clear focus/sense of awareness

- Lovers of nature, harmony, and inner beauty

- Introspective and (sometimes) introverted

- Highly attuned senses and strong intuition

- Warm-hearted with qualities of giving, selflessness, service, and generosity.

- Magnetic to energy vampires and attracting narcissists

- Very good listeners

- Artists, creatives, and dreamers

- Rich emotional worlds and great storytellers

- Deep desires for love and affection

- Function at a much higher frequency than others emotionally

- Comfort in abstract realms

- Nurturing, caregivers and natural counselors

- Overwhelmed in intimate relationships

- Time in nature to restore and replenish energy is essential

- Inspirational energy

HSP's and HIS's can unlock their empath nature much easier than people who are not empathically inclined. Highly sensitive people have an innate natural empathy due to the way they interact with the world. Their sensitivities to external influence, therefore, can be *alchemized and integrated* in a way that is beneficial, just like the empath.

Highly sensitive introverts too are already well on their way to becoming an empath, to *evolving* their unique way of perceiving and experiencing the world.

Meditation, mantras, mindfulness, and sound therapy are significant ways to access one's empathic nature. Through these activities, the sensitivities of the HS's can be *harnessed*, connected to in a controlled way, and *understood* in a way that is self- developing and self-mastering. Through meditation, mantras, and mindfulness, for example, the mind can be *reconditioned* and *retaught* to view things in a certain light. People, situations, experiences, and environments can all be *redefined* and levels of awareness *realigned*.

For example, instead of viewing loud noises as traumatic, harmful or disruptive, a highly sensitive can change the way they perceive it by adapting it to a *learning experience*. The beautiful, empathic qualities of the empathically inclined mind can therefore be activated, allowing for philosophical thought, introspection and *openness to new information and ideas*. Sensory stimuli thus become a part of life, as opposed to feeling separate and disconnected from it.

Life itself is an illusion. Reality is only real to the energy, intention, and substance we give it. We all experience life and daily situations from our own unique way of perceiving. So, if the highly sensitive people are *attuned* to experiencing life in a reflective and introverted way, why not use this to one's advantage? It can be *transformed* into a blessing.

The same is true for highly sensitive introverts; they are naturally *wired* to see life in an *energetically connected* way, connected to a reality of hidden feelings, emotions and impressions. Tuning in to their natural empathy, therefore, comes very easily with the right tools, techniques, and *awareness*. Sensitivity is a gift, and through self-development and self-mastery practices, both the HSI and HSP can thrive and survive, just like the empath.

Practical Techniques and Exercises

Before we begin, it is important to know that there is an abundance of information, research, and scientific studies available on the web to support and validitate the areas explored below. Of course, as an empath you experience through *feeling* and actually connecting to life-enhancing techniques and exercises! Unlike many non-empathic people who over-rationalize things out of existence (literally) you are *highly intuitive* and *experience* life's blessings and gifts, and on a very real level.

For these reasons, we have included just one scientific study as research for (some) of the areas delved into below; otherwise, this would read as a scientific research book, and this is about *connecting* to your superpowers! If you are feeling particularly 'non- empathic' and analytical, you can always research the science behind the substance in your own time.

1. Mindfulness: A study demonstrated by Harvard University showed how mindfulness can lead to positive change in the brain in depressed people.[2]("Harvard researchers study how mindfulness may change the brain in depressed patients," 2019). There has been much research conducted into mindfulness to show the range of benefits and effects in a number of different health areas.

2. Mantras/Affirmations: An article shared by *Psychology Today* shows how affirmations, which are similar to mantras, can change neurological activity in the brain and thus have a positive effect on mood, emotions and levels of thought and perception.[3] ("To

---

[2] Harvard researchers study how mindfulness may change the brain in depressed patients. (2019). Retrieved from https://news.harvard.edu/gazette/story/2018/04/harvard-researchers-study-how-mindfulness-may-change-the-brain-in-depressed-patients/

[3] To Affirm or Not Affirm?. (2019). Retrieved from https://www.psychologytoday.com/gb/blog/embodied-wellness/201704/affirm-or-not-

Affirm or Not Affirm?," 2019)

3. Sound: A fascinating study shared by the *National Center for Biotechnology Information* found that sound waves and mantras increased plant growth and also had a positive effect on human beings.[4] (Karnick, 2019)

4. Energy/chi: *Stanford Medicine* (Stanford University) actually conducted a study with Tai Chi Master to test the validity of chi and the results led one of the research associate's to state "it was fascinating" after finding that 'Master Li' possessed the ability to control his own body temperature. Furthermore, the effects of chi were shown directly on a thermography magnetic resonance imaging responsible for measuring biophysical changes.[5] ("Tai chi master studied for power to control body," 2019)

For many people, seeing is believing; yet, for an empath with such a heightened sense of sensitivity to the subtle world of energy, and an intrinsic *knowing*, a lot of this comes naturally

---

affirm

[4] Karnick, C. (2019). EFFECT OF MANTRAS ON HUMAN BEINGS AND PLANTS. Retrieved from https://www.ncbi.nlm.nih.gov/pmc/articles/PMC3336746/

[5] Tai chi master studied for power to control body. (2019). Retrieved from https://med.stanford.edu/news/all-news/2008/05/tai-chi-master-studied-for-power-to-control-body.html

to you. Connecting to the methods below, therefore, can not only enhance your own life but can also allow you to be a wayshower and positive influence on other people's lives. As stated earlier, you truly are inspirational and this is why it is essential to embrace your empathy and the gifts that accompany.

Let's now look at how to do so.

Meditation

As highly sensitive people and introverts are naturally in tune with the *inner worlds*, taking time to meditate can connect one powerfully to their own source of personal power. Quantum physicists have found that within every atom is virtually 99.9% space, which means everything in the universe is essentially empty space! Physical reality, therefore, becomes defined by the thoughts, feelings, and emotions we give them.

Meditation can be used to change the 'story' and the realities created in one's life.

Here are some forms of meditation to try and incorporate in daily life:

- *Transcendental meditation: transcending* the state of one's mind into a blissful, almost eutrophic and heavenly way of perceiving and experiencing the world.

- *Mindful meditation* (as explored in the next point)

- *Silent meditation*: being silent and present within oneself to explore and understand thoughts, feelings and belief patterns, and to make sense of any situation or experience present in life.

- *Focused meditation*: contemplating on any chosen topic or intention.

To begin with, any of these meditative exercises, start by finding your quiet place. This can be in your own private room or in a nature spot somewhere. The key is to practice, to begin with, somewhere you won't be disturbed. Once you can take control of your thoughts and your own inner happiness and contentment, you will find these exercises comes as easy as breathing!

When in your nature spot or quiet place, get comfortable and sit down cross-legged with your eyes closed. If you have access to incense, essential oils or special resins like Frankincense then perfect. Music can also be used to enhance meditation as described earlier (nature sounds, bird songs, whale and dolphin sounds, rainwater, Tibetan singing bowls and chimes, or mantra music and 'om'ing for a specific intent!)

Start breathing and coming into yourself. Focus your awareness on your breath, your body, and your inner state.

Any thoughts, distractions of strong emotions should be allowed to flow through you effortlessly. Remember: *what you resist persists*. Make peace with the uncomfortable feelings and stay focused on your breath. Once you begin to feel calm inside and reach a steady flow, apply any of the intentions you wish. Each unique meditation practice will have noticeable results which, over time, will lead to some incredible sensations and experiences.

Of course, make empathy one of those intentions!

Mindfulness

Mindfulness is becoming aware of the empty space and the thoughts and impressions inside. By practicing mindfulness, *being mindful*, conscious and developing awareness, our thoughts become more clear and an inner peace and sense of bliss results.

When we are mindful, we are paying attention to our thoughts. Instead of being the boat, aimlessly drifting around the sea, we become the engine, the compass, and the captain. We steer our lives in the right direction.

Mindfulness can be as simple as contemplation, meditation or (healthy) introspection. Being conscious of our thoughts and impressions allows us to break down any negative or detrimental thought patterns, processes, and conditioning into a way of perceiving which is in harmony with ourselves, others and the natural world. HIS's and HSP's therefore no longer feel separate or receive pain from those distractions and sensitivities and instead experience life with an inner calm and understanding.

Mindfulness can help with all aspects related to being highly sensitive. The best exercises to integrate for self- development are 'mindful meditation on empathy' and 'empathic mindfulness.'

Mindful meditation on empathy is meditating on mindfulness with accessing one's empathic nature as an *intent*. All meditation and healing exercises can be used to develop mindfulness with increased and integrated empathy as a goal, such as nature sounds, sound therapy, Reiki, mantras, and transcendental meditation. Just as our thoughts affect, create and shape space, setting your intention to enhance the empathic nature within can have some powerful results.

Empathic mindfulness is going about your daily life with the *specific intention and focused awareness of being empathic*. Embodying an empath nature will come naturally once you have begun including meditation as a daily practice. If you begin to become anxious, nervous or fearful in any way when in social situations, just remember how powerful your mind is. Empathic mindfulness will help you remember that you are a creator of your world, and no one can inflict harm unless you allow them to. Once you begin to find your flow and *actively shape the world around* you will realize just how special and powerful you are.

Mantras

Mantras are essentially a word or phrase repeated for effect, such as '*sensitivity is a gift, sensitivity is a gift; sensitivity is a gift.*' They can be spoken, sung, hummed or thought and can be used with meditation, as a *mindfulness mantra* or simply when walking about in day-to-day.

Try and include mantras daily which enhance and appreciate your *empathic gifts, intuition and enhanced ability to tune in to your senses.* Sing, hum or speak them wherever you go or take the time to create a sacred space and align with a mantra practice. You can get creative with your mantras. Always remember *the power of your intention and mind to shape physical matter.*

Your sensitivity is a gift and transforming it into empathy through mantras is a very effective way to develop the empath nature.

Sound therapy

As you are aware by now, sound can be used to change neurological activity and structures in the brain. Because our mind is affected by sound this, in turn, affects our emotions (as explored in chapter two). Using sound therefore to develop the empath nature can not only be extremely beneficial and powerful, but can also be very fun and stimulating!

When our brain's neurotransmitters pick up on certain sounds and frequencies, our consciousness is affected. Extending beyond the mental plane and mind, thoughts and impressions in the immediate now, the effect sound has on consciousness also relates to our *beliefs and subconscious programming*. In essence, sound therapy can change the structure of neurons to re*shape* and re*create* our core level programming. It is fascinating stuff.

Sound therapy encompasses a wide range of tools and outlets however the fundamental point is that you remember your intention. Focus your awareness and energy on *developing, integrating and enhancing your empathic tendencies*, and make a conscious effort to alchemize your sensitivities into empathy.

Various forms of sound therapy:

- *Nature Sounds* including bird song, rainwater, forest

sounds, whale and dolphin songs and waves crashing against the shore. All of these have a calming influence and can be used for study, meditation, contemplative activities and connecting to the natural world to enhance empathic qualities.

- *Shamanic drumming and/or tribal drumming*. Drumming acts as the universal heartbeat and can be used to synchronize your breathing, journey inside oneself, and to enter a trance state for healing, insight and subconscious encounters.

- *Shamanic journeying* can take you on an inner journey and open you up to wisdom, special insights, and connect you to both heart and higher self (the highest possible vibrational aspect of yourself).

- *Tibetan singing bowls, bells, and chimes* are used by monks and by many in the spiritual community to reach wholeness/healing and access transcendental inner states. They can be used directly in meditation and also combined to om practices.

- *Om-ing*. Speaking, singing, humming, or thinking om. Om is the universal sound of creation and can bring great healing on many levels. It can connect you to your heart, higher self, and inner empathic state through intentions.

- **Gongs and musical instruments** can be used in a sound journey where one explores many aspects of their own mind, emotional body, physical sensations, and soul.

- **Sound journeying** is usually a multi-dimensional experience and can lead to heightened sensitivity while simultaneously grounding one within.

- **Silence or silent meditation** is, in itself, a form of sound therapy. It is also known as contemplative meditation.

Reiki

Reiki, or Usui Reiki, is a form of natural healing introduced and developed by Dr. Mikau Usui in Japan in 1922. Dr. Usui spent 21 days and nights meditating on a mountain with no food, solely getting his energy from spirit. He did this because he wanted to experience *enlightenment* and access the deepest parts of his soul and psyche. On day 21, he had a profound enlightenment experience and decided to travel back down from the mountain. On his way down, he fell and hurt his big toe. When he reached out his hands, to his amazement, he could heal; his hands had become *healing hands*, and he was able to *channel chi, the universal life-force energy.*

Dr. Usui further went on to develop the Usui Reiki system of natural healing. Nowadays, a series of techniques are taught to heal both self and others, yet the principles are universal and relate to many other schools of thought and healing modalities. The gift he received from spirit is universal and can, therefore, be accessed by everyone. We all have healing hands!

Highly sensitives and empaths, however, can tune in to the *natural life-force energy*, the chi, or Reiki much easier than others. For some it is literally as simple as meditating and *setting the intention to heal, to channel healing life-force energy.* Reiki is a beautiful practice to learn and can really help HS's ground their unique energy into the physical world.

Take a Reiki course with an established, experienced and certified master. The best teachers are those who are also trained in shamanism and naturally shamanic-ally inclined, or at least learn one-on-one, so you have a personal and unique experience with Reiki and attuning to your gifts (groups are not recommended). For now, however, try the exercises in the first two chapters to connect to your inner chi for healing power. Allowing the energy to flow through you and setting your intention to open your palms—your healing hands—will not only help with confidence but will also have a range of benefits.

Some of the benefits of Reiki include:

- Assisting the immune system to help heal disease and illness

- Aiding the nervous system to help with stress, tension, and/or anxiety

- Increases vitality and life-force energy allowing for a healthy flow of chi through your mind,body and emotional centers

- DNA and cellular healing and reprogramming

- Balances emotions and relieves emotional blockages

- Helps heal traumas, ancestral wounds, and assists in karmic healing

- Enhances all aspects relating to psychic phenomena such as the ability to connect to dream states, third eye opening, intuition, lucid dream and astral projection, extra-sensory perception, channeling and connecting to higher wisdom and power

- Creative expression and evolved imaginative abilities

- Helps with repetitive thought or emotional patterns

- Induces peace, inner calmness, and clarity

- Aids in a variety of physical ailments

- Can heal sexual issues and increase kundalini flow

- Connects you to the heart and your 'super' consciousness

This list is not exclusive!

Holistic Therapies & Healing

Just like with Reiki, there are a lot of different courses, therapies, and healing modalities you can learn to develop and ground the elements of your personality which make you empathic (if you are a HSP or HIS). If you are an empath, these therapies can ground and stabilize your empathic nature further, taking your *natural gifts* to the next level.

These include but are not limited to:

- Crystal therapy

- Psychoanalysis

- Herbalism/herbs for holistic well-being

- Acupuncture

- Acupressure

- Reflexology

- Aromatherapy

- Shiatsu

- Holistic massage

- Trigger point therapy

- Shamanic healing

- Sound therapy

- Hypnosis/ hypnotherapy

- Indian head massage

- Dream therapy

- Yoga and tantric yoga

- Tai chi

- Chi kung/Qi gong

- Cranial-sacral massage

This list is not exclusive, but the point to bring into awareness is that western medicine and healthcare is not the only way to achieve health. Paradoxically, therapies such as the ones named above actually provide a more *holistic* approach to treatment and in many can heal the root cause, as opposed to just the symptoms. Holistic-healing modalities have an encompassing approach to achieving *wholeness* as they consider the human being as a complete and complex individual. In this respect, they are specifically effective for sensitives as they benefit the mind, the emotions, the body, and the spirit.

Some of them specifically specialise in hidden emotions, traumas or sensitivities relating to the empathic nature, such as cranial-sacral therapy for wounds in sexuality and deeply buried emotions, or crystal therapy for energy blockages in the auric (energy) field.

If you feel inclined to learn and train in any of the above, either for self or to evolve the wisdom, teachings and practical applications into a service to help others, the School of Natural Health Sciences is an established, professional and friendly online college with a range of holistic therapies, which is highly recommended.

Nature

Nothing is arguably better for the highly sensitive person or introvert than nature. Nature recharges emotions, replenishes energy and heals on *all levels*. It can bring feelings of love, warmth, and protection, and generally wraps one in a massive ethereal hug. Nature is healing.

For the sensitive person, introvert or empath, spending time alone or with just a few close friends is one of the most enjoyable things to do. Not only does the natural world replenish and recharge one's energy, but it also acts as an emotional restart. This is because empaths take on other's emotions, stories and burdens, even without being consciously aware. So, spending time in nature allows the empath to return to their true nature, center and personal alignment.

Some of the benefits of nature include:

- Increased energy levels;

- Emotional 'reboot';

- Centering and alignment;

- Mental clarity and clearing of old 'stories';

- Improved physical health and vitality;

- Normalizing circadian rhythms;

- Improving hormone-related symptoms;

- Protecting the body from electromagnetic interference and harsh energies;

- Protecting and cleansing the aura (the invisible energy field around you);

- Increased healing;

- Sleep enhancement;

- Reduction of stress, anxiety and nervous tension;

- Increased cognitive functioning;

- Creative genius and imagination; and

- Increased spatial awareness.

To connect more to your empath nature, take any one of the meditation exercises in this chapter and practice in nature. The natural air and universal life force around will amplify your ability to perform and perfect the practices and will naturally enable you to feel more in tune with yourself.

Your superpowers are well on their way.

Chapter 4

Down the Rabbit Hole

Psychology of the Self: Jung's Archetypes

Carl Jung was a Swiss psychiatrist and one of the founders of modern psychology. He came up with a set of *universal archetypes* of *the Self*, which are aspects of the whole human being, relating to everyone on earth and everyone who ever will be. These archetypes are aspects of the *collective consciousness*.

His archetypes were created from his explorations of the collective unconscious through different religions of the east and west, mythology, and alchemy. He believed archetypes manifested themselves in dreams through symbols and figures, and these dreams could be used to understand daily life. Once activated, they could *unlock* a specific frequency or energy type within the person, specifically associated with the archetype.

When exploring what it means to be an empath, I believe it is essential to look to the *subconscious aspects* of ourselves for understanding and integration. Carl Jung's offer a certain type of guidance and insight which can be used to connect to those 'hidden' and behind-the-scenes influences that shape and create the empath as we understand. They can also help define what it means to have empathy.

As our brains are transmitters and receivers of consciousness, in dreams we can learn a great deal about our impressions and beliefs, and gain insight and wisdom for everyday reality. Let's explore each of these universal archetypes and how they relate to the wonderful gift of being an empath.

The Persona

The persona is the image you present to the world in daily life. It is your mask or sense of image, such as 'the caring empath,' 'the crazy scientist,' 'the gifted artist' or 'the helpful healer.' The term persona literally comes from the Latin 'mask' and in dreams is represented by *the Self*, a character you know is you.

Jung referred to the persona as 'the conformity archetype' and believed it essential in personal development. Depending on where you are at in your own journey of transformation, empaths often feel they have to put on a mask and be something for everyone. Your true nature can often be replaced with a 'persona,' an image you feel you have to reflect to the world. This is because of your natural tendency toward *sacrifice*.

By now, you are aware you empaths have extraordinary gifts. Combined with this and your genuine desire to do good, however innate and sometimes uncontrollable feelings of shame, guilt and suppression are often present. *Why should I be allowed to shine in my strongest light when others around me aren't? Is it selfish that I am now fully in my power, connected to and in tune with my natural and beautiful gifts?*

These are some of the questions you find yourself dealing with even once you have done the inner work and begun your journey to self-mastery. Concerns and struggles lie beyond the mundane and you re*cognize* that your purpose is beyond the 'I,' the selfish and ego reality many people on planet Earth are operating at. Of course, in its positive expression, as defined by some of the archetypes shared above, the characters we embody are ourselves (the Self) in its truest light, in our *highest possible frequency*. ('The helpful healer,' 'the caring empath...')

Many empaths today struggle with stepping fully into their true persona based on the judgments of the outside world. It can be very hard to stay centered, aligned and fully connected to one's truth when your nature is naturally to appease and sacrifice for the benefit of others.

But the goal of the empath is to heal and help and to bring others up. Once you fully realize this and truly come to terms with the truth that *we are all one*, you will realize it is detrimental and harmful to not stand in your light and shine your gifts. Devolving helps no one!

We can look to our personas, therefore, and the characters which present themselves to us in dreams, which we know our symbolic of the self, to help understand and accept our empathic nature. As with everything in life, balance is essential; dreams are able to communicate to us through symbols and direct messages where and how our empathy is being used positively, either for the benefit of self or of others; and when it may be subconsciously harming us in some way.

For example, if you were to dream that you were in a crowded place, holding on to your favorite toy as a child feeling lost, confused and alone, this dream message would be suggesting that either 1. you still have yet to become grounded, centered and strong within as you feel lost and alone in public spaces and with groups of people, or 2. you are too empathic, and your strong empathic personality is disconnecting you from those around you (the childhood toy represents a feeling of home, emotional connection and comfort, and feminine energy, strongly associated with the empath nature. Feeling lost, confused and alone suggests the dream is showing you a negative aspect of yourself, or a part of self which needs healing).

The Shadow

The shadow is those aspects of self that you wish to deny. It is the hidden, repressed and rejected parts of your personality, character or being which you perceive as *ugly*. They can represent fear, anger or weakness, and usually manifest as desires and memories which one simply does not wish to accept or integrate. Animal instincts and sexuality are integral parts of the collective shadow and shadow aspect of an empath (we explore sexuality in-depth later). In dreams, the shadow can represent itself as a 'lowly creature,' such as a dwarf, or an animal representing primal and instinctual instincts, such as a tiger.

The general rule is that the stronger we identify with our persona, the more we deny other aspects of ourselves. So how does this show itself as an empath?

Let's take any one of our potential personas: an animal activist who dedicates daily love and affection to animals in shelters; a charity worker who is constantly engaged in projects and activities to make other's lives better; a care or support worker who helps the elderly or children in need on a daily basis; a healer or therapist who devotes endless hours to others with the sole intention of bringing healing and wholeness to humanity and planet Earth's collective energy field; or a compassionate meditator who spends their life dedicated to daily mantras for world love and peace.

Each one of these are dedicated to helping others in some way. They pour copious amounts of time, love and energy into a goal, commitment or project which will enrich another's life. (It is important to remember that we empaths do this because we genuinely want to—there is no *inherently* unhealthy sacrifice in these choices and paths). But, an empath often goes too far. You focus so much on another that you *forget yourself*. A strive for perfection, an integral characteristic of the empath, means that you may subconsciously neglect your private life and personal joys, pleasures, and abundance. You *reject* the parts of self which make you whole.

Reoccurring themes that are often present in empath's life:

- A suppression of sex, love, and desire;

- A suppression of intimacy, self-love, and connection;

- A suppression of money, abundance, and financial prosperity;

- A suppression of health, personal development, and self-mastery; and

- A suppression of material bliss, new opportunities, and living one's   dreams.

These can be seen as *shadow aspects of the empath*, as in the process of always wishing to be there for others and do something good in the world one's personal needs and prosperity are sacrificed and repressed.

Looking at the shadow aspects of oneself can be a beautiful process as it allows you to delve deep into the positive associations of your character; the helpfulness, the giving, the generosity, and caring empathy, and those aspects which are detrimental. Self-sacrifice, suppression, and neglect serve no one and one of the key life lessons you will learn is that you cannot give all of yourself away. Your time, love, energy, gifts and resources are very important!

Furthermore, the shadow can actually be dangerous when not recognized as denying something leads to its greater persistence. We all have light and dark, good and evil, and opposing forces within us; therefore, by coming to terms with our own shadows and *the collective shadow aspects of the empath nature* we can live life in a state of harmony, balance, and contentment, truly connected to and at one with our unique gifts.

The Anima/Animus

These are female and male aspects of yourself, respectively. Everyone possesses both feminine and masculine attributes.

Therefore, the anima and animus are not limited to being a woman or man. Empaths can naturally be seen as more feminine as the *gift of empathy* is to be able to connect with others on an emotional level, which is a feminine quality.

Regarding of being an empath, when the anima or animus is unconscious and not seen, understood or accepted, we tend to *project* it outward onto others. As explored in 'The Main Struggles of an Empath,' one of the main ways this manifests is in relationships, specifically romantic and sexual relationships. Once you begin to have a synergistic relationship with your own inner-empath nature, only then can you *reflect* it out to the world in a way that is harmonious and healthy.

Projection thus transforms into reflection, and you mirror the beautiful innate qualities of the empath nature, instead of suppressing them (the latter resulting in projecting your shadow onto others).

The Divine Child

The divine child is your truest self in its purest form in that it represents your innocence, your sense of vulnerability and your helplessness. It also, however, symbolizes your goals, dreams and aspirations, and your highest potential. In dreams, it is represented by a child, baby, or infant.

Now, regarding being an empath, we can see this universal archetype as a fundamental part to the empath's journey. They can arguably be seen as one and the same; therefore, if you are looking for an archetype to connect to and embody in your meditations, the divine child is the perfect one.

This is because empaths are literally all those things Carl Jung defined it as (the divine child). Innocence, vulnerability and helplessness, goals and dreams, aspirations and highest potential: this is ultimately the journey of an empath!

Empaths can be seen as vulnerable and helpless due to their weakness. Simply put, before you begin to strengthen your aura and take the steps toward turning your gifts into powers, you are weak. You merge with others unconsciously and take on things which do not belong to you. You also attract narcissists and energy vampires and, generally speaking, have no sense of self, boundaries or protection. This is due to *your innocence*; you see the world and all its inhabitants as a reflection of you. You receive great joy and inner peace from being with nature or taking time to contemplate near animals, so you see the world as a mirror.

Yet, this beautiful innocence is simultaneously your vulnerability and helplessness (until you find yourself!) Not everyone is as kind, warm-hearted or intuitive as you, and there are some really cold and mean-spirited people in the world today. Once you have centered and aligned yourself, however, the *inner beauty* you possess can lead you to your most positive expressions and highest potential.

So your dreams, goals and aspirations are what result after you have embraced your unique vulnerability, innocence, and gifts as an empath, and taken steps to manifest your true path. What is your path?

In essence, there is no one true path as even among empaths you still have your own *unique personal blueprint, your individual soul print*. Assuming, however, that you are in fact destined to follow 'the path of the empath,' these manifestations will inevitably present itself as hopes, goals and aspirations which lie in the realms of spirit, creativity, charity, service, animal welfare, environmentalism, healing, helping, or caring of some kind (we will explore this in more detail later).

The Wise Old Man

This archetype is pretty self-explanatory. In dreams, he is represented by a masculine figure of some sort; a father, teacher or a masculine-type authority figure. The purpose of the wise old man is to offer insight, direction, and guidance.

Through dream work, working consciously with our dreams,

we can explore the subconscious realms and actively ask for wisdom, guidance, and assistance. Dreams can be seen as gateways to the soul and can be used for help in everyday life.

The Great Mother

Like the wise old man, the great mother is the feminine aspect of your subconscious who can be called on for help. She is the great nurturer and manifests in dreams as a grandmother, mother, fairy godmother or any powerful and nurturing female figure.

This archetype is very important when it comes to exploring our nature as the negative expression and association of the great mother is the *witch*. Now, we are not talking about good witches, those real medicine women or magical, crystal-loving fairy types, but the 'evil' type. This type of witch is the terrifying, green goblin, stereotypical black-cloaked witch with an evil face. She represents dominance, death and seduction, and is very important in embracing the shadow elements of ourselves, that we may wish to deny.

If the witch shows up in a dream, it is a signal that we are *rejecting or suppressing* the aspect she relates to. *Themes of death and destruction, seduction and sexuality are an integral part of life,* even if not acting upon them (sex, desire, lust, etc.). So, like with the shadow, ignoring a part of our nature in pursuit of perfection or to be everything for everyone creates an accumulation of suppressed energy to occur (which manifests itself as the *evil witch*).

Nightmares, therefore, show us just how important it is, especially as an empath who feels everything so deeply and takes on others pain, emotions, and traumas, to *accept and integrate* those aspects of the self we do not necessarily wish to embody. It is only when we truly do this that we can become the best versions of ourselves and use our gifts for good.

The Trickster

As the name suggests, the trickster is the practical joker of the collective consciousness archetypes. He may present himself in dreams if you have taken yourself too seriously, misjudged or over-reacted to a situation or person. Now, as an *empath*, this is a very important archetype to be aware of!

Empaths genuinely *do* take themselves very seriously. An empath feels so deeply and in an attempt to be healing, helping and there for those in need one can often not incorporate the wit and humor necessary in some situations. Of course, in a lot of situations where empathy is called for, depth and heart and soul-level sharing is beautiful and beneficial, but in many other cases a friend or loved one does just want some good old-fashioned giggles or banter to cheer them up.

The trickster archetype, therefore, can be learned about, integrated and meditated on to enhance the missing qualities in your life. His energy is not specifically masculine as laughter, wit and humor can be very feminine, too; however, relating to the empath nature we can suggest that this archetype is effective for increasing masculine energy and all aspects relating to light-heartedness.

The Ego

The ego is one of the main archetypes of the personality and is the center of consciousness. It is the 'I,' the aspect of self that is central in daily life. It is the part that relates to the psyche and all things personal, personal experiences, lessons, and learnings throughout the entire human journey. The other part of the psyche is the unconscious.

So how does this relate to us empaths?

The Self

The self can be seen as the most important archetype in that is the *whole personality*, the totality of it. It is *centeredness, the union of the conscious and unconscious* and embodies the balance and harmony of the opposing elements of the psyche. In dreams, the self is depicted as a circle, mandala, crystal or stone (impersonally), or as a royal couple, divine child, or some other symbol of divinity such as Christ, Buddha, or other great spiritual teachers (personally).

These symbols of the self are all representations of *wholeness, completeness, unification, and reconciliation of opposites*, therefore, can be connected to when discovering the deepest workings of the empath psyche.

As you are aware, empaths are kind, compassionate, sensitive, spiritually-oriented, and can merge with another on a deep level. You enjoy nature, are warm-hearted and have a powerful natural intuition. You can use this gift for healing, raising other people's light and to bring harmony, balance and unity in any situation. Becoming in tune with yourself therefore in your *ultimate and unified expression*, without repressions, suppressions or denial, will allow you to thrive and experience life in its fullest, deepest, and most joyous way.

The self, your whole and integrated personality which can be seen as *self-mastered*, is your inner guide to help navigate you through all of life's queries, concerns and problems. It is essentially your superpower! By taking the necessary steps and following all the techniques, exercises and tips shared throughout this book you can live your best life full of joy, content, and abundance, and achieve your highest possible vibration (and maintain it!)

Healers, Therapist & Spiritual Intuitives

As briefly explored throughout these chapters, empaths have a healing nature. You are kind, possess incredible listening skills, operate at a much higher frequency emotionally than many, and naturally find yourself gravitating toward those that need your help in some way. For this reason, empaths are *natural healers, therapists, counselors, and spiritual intuitives.* You also make *incredible artists, musicians, creatives and visionaries*, as explored earlier. You have the gift of sight, you can see things beyond the surface and, when expressed creatively, can be used to produce some genius and *extra*ordinary ideas.

Regarding healing, due to your ability to merge with another, feel their feelings and connect with them on such a deep level, this is incredibly powerful if you choose to ground it into a career such as the holistic or healing fields. Your *advanced levels of intuition and awareness* also mean you would thrive in any of the metaphysical and spiritual fields, such as tarot and psychic readings, Reiki and energy healing, and spiritual counseling.

Combined with your love of the natural world and connecting

to others, empaths also are steered towards animal welfare, charity work, environmentalism and the caring, nursing or support fields.

Now, as everyone is on their own unique journey and only you will know what path and career is best for you, through working through all the techniques to connect to your superpowers in this book (and integrating them on a daily basis!), in this section we will explore how you can connect to your *inner archetypes* in daily life, without necessarily choosing to go into it as a life path (profession). Although you can and many do!

The Healer

As an empath, you naturally embody the inner healer archetype due to your ability to merge with others on a deep level. You can read and understand people beyond the norm, and have the ability of *scanning people's psyches* to see what is beyond the surface. You tune in to others' thoughts and inner vibrational frequency and can, therefore, use this as a gift for healing.

You can also sense the truth of another, knowing when they lie or are deceitful or simply if they are hiding something. This really helps when wishing to be *a channel for healing*, as many are often fearful, shy or anxious in some way to bring truth to

137

light. You naturally possess the ability to do this in a way which is both empathic, compassionate and assertive. Because you have such a warm and genuine heart and others feel your inner compassionate nature, it is very easy to connect to others and bring secrets or things that simply do not wish to be shared to the surface.

The world is full of judgment, delusions, and spite, and can sometimes be a hard and cold place. It is a great gift to be able to bring to the surface an embarrassing or shameful truth, yet you do this naturally with *compassion and an inner knowing*. This is ultimately the gift of the healer.

In addition to your mental, emotional and intuitive powers, as an empath, you also are more naturally in tune with your inner healer through *the physical ability to channel healing energy*. This is because of your connection to the natural world and an intrinsic love of nature. It is in nature where our chi—our universal life force energy—is restored and increased; therefore, through your powerful connection to nature and the subtler realms of existence, you naturally possess a gift that would allow you to develop and evolve your healing hands.

This can be used in any hands-on therapy or energy work such as in massage, Reiki, energy healing, working with oils and flower essences, herbs and any other touch therapies.

The Caregiver

Your heightened sensitivity can and often translates as compassion, consideration, care and understanding for others. This makes you are natural caregiver and, once again, you can feel what others are feeling in an uncanny way, which can even be seen as *supernatural*.

Because many of the elderly are nearing the end of their human journey and making their way back to spirit, your beautiful empathic gifts make you an excellent care worker, support assistant or volunteer with the elderly. You also connect to those with mental health issues, the disabled and children in a unique way, and often find yourself having strangers open up and talk to you about their problems. This is because empaths have an inner warmth and compassion which people get attracted to; they simply know even if they are not that empathic themselves.

Many empaths find themselves on a park bench or observing some animal or flower in an outside space, for example, and someone will come up and randomly start unloading their burdens or speaking about something mentally and philosophically stimulating. This is because your empathy is connected to your *heart chakra* and when you are in nature and in your true self, it glows divinely. You don't even necessarily have to try, as just being yourself and seeing the world in your own unique way attracts people to you.

For this reason, you are naturally one of the most caring, kind, generous and loving of people with your time, energy, and emotional wisdom.

The Counselor

Like with the caregiver inner archetype, you are a natural counselor. All the reasons above for you naturally representing both inner healer and inner caregiver, make you a remarkable person to talk to. People seek your advice and open up to you, and you have the wonderful ability to know things and see behind the surface. Combined with this is your incredible listening skills and ability to communicate emotional wisdom and insights effectively.

Just like snakes who can sense things through the vibrations emitted, you are able to *tune in* to another's aura, energy body and unseen emotions and connect to them, bringing them to the surface. This has so many implications as you can literally have a conversation with another person's cells and use that gift for healing or bringing insight to any mental, emotional, spiritual, physical or soul-level issue. Blockages, problems, unresolved traumas, repressed emotions, daily life concerns and karmic ties can all be *brought to light* and, as mentioned regarding your caregiver archetype, you do so in a way which is compassionate, patient and kind.

Empaths really are naturals of so many things!

The Animal Activist

Simply put, you love animals! You can relate to them; therefore, you would thrive in any profession or activity regarding helping animals. Animal welfare, dog sitting, dog grooming, volunteering time at your local cat shelter, helping at rescue centers, or going further and joining or starting campaigns which strive for animal rights—these are all in harmony with your nature.

Due to your deep-seated empathy and ability to connect to others and animals, empaths also make particularly good animal healers. Paths and abilities related are 'horse whisperers,' 'animal Reiki healers' and any of type of animal healer or whisperer. This is because you literally can speak to animals. You understand them and they understand you. This gift is on such a deep level that there are many who still perceive this idea and reality as crazy, but it is very real to you, and to the animal. Animals are intelligent, empathic, intuitive and compassionate creatures (most) and you see this.

When we recognize someone, we are re*cognizing* our minds, restructuring the neural pathways which allow us to see them in a connected and unified way. Because of your enhanced empathy and high-frequency emotional functioning, you possess gifts that many would have to train in, and even then, may not naturally have access to. You, therefore, could use and embrace your deep empathy with animals to assist in healing the animal queen and kingdoms, or at least develop your own personal connection to them further.

The Spiritual Intuitive or Psychic

As empaths possess such an evolved natural intuition, inner knowing and *vibration of spiritual and higher awareness*, it can be argued that you are meant to be a spiritual intuitive, psychic or healer. Your ability to pick up and tune in to others is the essence of what a psychic does and who they are, and there are a lot of people who could benefit from this gift.

Refer to the 'Shaman and Inner Seer' archetype in chapter two to better understand the spiritual and psychic aspect to your personality.

The Empath and Sexuality

As briefly explored in the first section of this book, sexuality is a major aspect to the path of the empath. Romantic and intimate sexual relationships tend to involve adequate amounts of pain and suffering early in life, as an empath attracts narcissists, abusers, and energy vampires into their auric field. They also attract oppressors and people who take advantage of their gentle natures.

When it comes to sexuality, empaths can be very submissive. This is understandable when we observe the romantic, sensitive, and intuitive nature of an empath. However, despite your advanced levels of intuition, when younger empaths simply aren't aware that they are empathic, they are not conscious of the types of partner they attract. This, of course, has a profound effect on future relationships.

Carl Jung's universal archetypes can help you to understand and integrate your sexuality fully, in a way that is healthy, balanced and loving to yourself. Unconscious wounds and traumas can often manifest in sexual partnerships; therefore, looking to and exploring your *shadow*, the 'dark' and hidden parts of yourself, will better help you make sense of them, accept them, and bring them into the light.

Traumas and Ancestral Wounds

As briefly discussed in chapter one, your traumas and ancestral wounds are issues that have grown with you since childhood. They are the *subconscious and repressed* aspects of yourself which are brought into adult relationships and can lead to some very painful and tricky experiences. Traumas and wounds also run deeper than this in that they are part of the collective psyche; they are universal.

So what does this mean as an empath?

As you naturally take on everyone else's things from their emotions to their moods, thoughts and inner being, this means that you are also at greater risk of absorbing other people's personal traumas. These are the traumas and wounds that have accumulated not only in this life, but in many.

Everyone has a unique soul print, a specific story, frequency and blueprint sole to that individual. As an empath, therefore, it is very easy to unconsciously connect to some of someone else's' deepest and most hidden unresolved traumas. The person themselves may not even be aware of them. They exist on a *soul level*, buried behind the surface.

So this takes us to one of your *super*powers and ultimately defines why empathy is such an incredible gift. Without even being aware, you naturally *tune in* to invisible and behind-the-scenes pains, traumas and wounds, and bring them to light.

Now, this is incredibly powerful and can be used for great benefit. If used correctly, with love, compassion, and kindness, you can become a real gem in someone's life! If used negatively however then one could say you are *abusing your power*, tuning in and connecting to this special empathic gift to either cause harm or to satisfy your own ego and sense of worth. The whole *intention* therefore of connecting to your superpower is to live with love, to live from the heart.

Before you can do this, however, there are personal traumas unique to the empath which need to be addressed. All the above is completely real and true. As an empath, you *can* connect either unconsciously or consciously to others hidden wounds and traumas to heal and be of assistance. But first, as with all empaths, you need to make sure you yourself are healed on all levels so you don't take on another's pain in a way that is detrimental to you. Otherwise, life will be a repetitive vicious cycle and you could be back at the beginning of your journey!

Let's look at the way trauma can manifest itself in life:

- Spending a lot of time alone, to an unhealthy extent

- Creating a dream world and escaping from reality (escapist behaviors/escapism)

- Addictions such as food, alcohol, tobacco, substance, drugs, television and   porn

- Self-consciousness and inability to speak your truth

- Repressing, denying or escaping from pain, blocking out real suffering

- Going within to the point of extreme introversion

- Not being able to connect, experience intimacy (platonic) or have intimate relationships

- Minor fears of public places, social gatherings and crowds

- Oversensitive in intimate relationships

- Attracting narcissists, energy vampires, and oppressive types

These, of course, link to the struggles of an empath, so if you find yourself experiencing any of the above, go back to the exercises at the beginning of this book (chapter one) to assist in the specific areas you need help with. You can also use any of the techniques in chapters two and three to aid in your healing journey.

As this topic is all about ancestral wounds, however, below is a very effective activity for clearing and releasing wounds, pains and karmic traumas on a soul level. This is specifically for self-mastery, once you feel balanced and aligned within and have integrated all the other daily practices and techniques for embracing your empathy as a gift and connecting to your inner power.

Chapter 5

Taking the Evolutionary Leap

Individual & Collective Consciousness: Does Our Unconscious Collective Mind Create the Empath, Or Do the Empath's Ways, Thoughts and Behaviors Shape the Collective?

This is a very interesting topic when exploring the nature of an empath. We have already delved deep into many different elements, perspectives, and school of thought; therefore, we should have an integrated understanding of the empathic nature and gifts of an empath in its entirety.

So is it the unconscious collective, our wounds, traumas, conditioning and collective experiences which create the empath? Or is it the powerful, loving and unique empathic ways which shape the collective?

Paradoxically, both are true, and there is no set-in-stone answer. The best way to explore this topic, therefore, is to look to the intention, the why and what this means. Without heart there would be no life; everything in the universe exists because of the vibrational frequency of love. Life is love; creation is love and the earth herself is loving, beautiful and abundant. The empath nature embodies this love.

As briefly explored, the empathic nature can be defined by the heart center, it is essentially its embodiment. Kindness, care, compassion; a love for mother earth and the natural world, and a deep-seated empathy is all intrinsic to the essence of the heart center. As the heart is the center, connecting both our *lower self and higher self*, it can be seen that the empath is the perfect representation of this.

Empaths are the perfect balance and unification of the lower self, emotions, a deep connection to the earth and all its inhabitants, feeling and birthing new ideas, insights and high power into the physical; and the higher self, intuition, connecting to spirit and unseen realms, dreams and an evolved emotional frequency. In relation to this question, it can, therefore, be seen that empaths both influence and affect the collective conscious and global energy field, and are a physical manifestation of it. The empath nature is literally to *tune in* and connect to something which is above and beyond the human ego and 'I' centered reality. Arguably, the ultimate way the collective can be seen (in its ideal form) is as an embodiment of love, unity, divinity and conscious global humanity.

Thus, through the empath's intentions, ways, beliefs and actions they *actively reshape and restructure the world*, and our subsequent collective conscious energy field. The beautiful gift of empathy and all its real-life implications and applications enable empaths all over the world to have a powerful effect and be catalysts for love, self-development, healing, and evolution and enhanced gifts of compassion and creative expression.

Taking the Evolutionary Leap: How Empathy and Sensitivity Can Be Used to Enhance Extra-Sensory Perception, Unlock Spiritual Gifts and Activate Consciousness

This takes us to the empath's superpowers. We have already explored various elements to this topic throughout these chapters, so continuing from the last section to this final chapter.

It can be suggested that the empath nature is the ultimate journey in the evolutionary leap. Unlike the highly sensitive who can become overloaded with their unique sensitivities, the empath has fine-tuned and *become one* with them. They then use these sensitives and empathic gifts to be healers, channels, guides and way-showers for others. Even if one does not ground their gifts into a structured profession, they are still using them on a daily basis.

This, of course, activates consciousness. When one individual accesses certain codons of information or connects, on a real level, to a specific archetype, a ripple effect is created. *The vibrational frequency of the element being explored becomes activated*, allowing others across the globe easier access. Through unlocking spiritual gifts, spirit itself becomes more accessible and because we are all connected, more awaken to their own inner gifts.

An empaths individual journey, therefore, is intrinsically connected to the collective journey, and this is why it is essential for all empaths around the world to wake up and step fully into their beautiful empathic power, letting go of the old stories of over-sensitivity, low self-esteem, and depressive tendencies and *embracing* their *super*powers.

Everything begins in the now.

Unconditional Love and Acceptance

As you are aware by now, a huge part of the empath's journey is about love and acceptance. Empaths have that strong tendency to *strive for perfection, aim to be their best* and *be there for everyone* in every single way. In the pursuit of purity and perfection, you neglect your own personal needs and desires.

In this respect, it can ultimately be seen that a*ccepting and integrating the shadow fully*, the aspects of one's self and the empath personality that you would rather not embrace or accept, is the final achievement in the goal to self-mastery and *alchemizing your sensitivity into superpowers*. As an empath, you have some remarkable gifts, some of which many on this planet spend days, weeks and even years aiming to perfect. Yet with you, they are inherent and completely natural.

Before we can fully step into any one of our chosen or given roles, it is essential that we practice unconditional love for ourselves, not just for everyone else. Loving you and treating yourself with the respect, kindness and care you deserve allows you to be the beautiful empathic being you wish to fully be. Self-criticism, taking oneself too seriously, sacrificing your own joys and peace for others; these just simply won't work. Only when you are full and completely recharged can you shine your light and gifts out to others, and it all starts with self-love and acceptance.

As an empathic child, you were almost certainly told to stop being so sensitive or were shamed in some way for being so. You most likely felt like you couldn't be yourself or had to suppress your feelings because they were 'wrong.' You probably didn't have parents or guardians who could meet you on your level, regardless of how much they loved you.

So you brought these wounds into adulthood, and they manifested themselves as problems and pains in your relationships. But now you are strong, wise and centered. ***You are a beautiful, divine, caring and empathic soul***, and by now I hope you realize this. All of those childhood traumas, unconscious wounds and patterns of behavior no longer play a part in your life. You are now free to shine your superpowers out to the world!

It begins with unconditional love and acceptance.

Conclusion

This book aims to explore the various elements of what it means 'to be empathic' in a way which is relatable, insightful, and healing. The practical techniques and exercises throughout will help you connect to your *inner empath*, transcending the 'shadow' aspects to the empath personality and bringing great self-development and understanding, wholeness and integration.

This book is unique in that it explores many schools of thought, and merges it into an encompassing and loving, detailed account which can be used in everyday life.

Empathy is a superpower, not a sensitivity

References

Auditory Beat Stimulation and its Effects on Cognition and Mood States. (2015). Retrieved from https://www.ncbi.nlm.nih.gov

Harvard researchers study how mindfulness may change the brain in depressed patients. (2019). Retrieved from https://news.harvard.edu/gazette/story/2018/04/harvard-researchers-study-how-mindfulness-may-change-the-brain-in-depressed-patients/

Karnick, C. (2019). EFFECT OF MANTRAS ON HUMAN BEINGS AND PLANTS. Retrieved from https://www.ncbi.nlm.nih.gov/pmc/articles/PMC3336746/

Tai chi master studied for power to control body. (2019). Retrieved from https://med.stanford.edu/news/all-news/2008/05/tai-chi-master-studied-for-power-to-control-body.html

To Affirm or Not Affirm?. (2019). Retrieved from https://www.psychologytoday.com/gb/blog/embodied-wellness/201704/affirm-or-not-affirm

Notes

www.ingramcontent.com/pod-product-compliance
Lightning Source LLC
Chambersburg PA
CBHW051348280526
45784CB00007B/2865